HERE

HERE WE STAND

Justification by Faith Today

J. I. Packer   M. Butterworth   S. Motyer
J. Atkinson   G. L. Bray   G. Carey
D. H. Wheaton

HODDER AND STOUGHTON
LONDON   SYDNEY   AUCKLAND   TORONTO

British Library Cataloguing in Publication Data

Here we stand: justification by faith today.
  1. Justification
  I. Packer, J. I.
  234'.7   BT764.2

  ISBN 0 340 34502 0

PREFACE

This set of essays celebrates the golden jubilee of Oak Hill Theological College. The writers are past or present members of the teaching faculty, apart from Professor Atkinson, who examined for the College's BA degree.

I myself taught at Oak Hill as long ago as the academic year 1948–9. I had just graduated and was the youngest man in the place. Everyone was very kind. Years later, when an article in the *Oak Leaf* chronicled the inanities of two pseudo-pundits named John Clott and Dr Cracker, I saw that I was, after a fashion, remembered. It was, however, an unexpected honour and delight to be asked to share in this book.

The subject of justification was chosen before the invitation came to me. I am free, therefore, to say that I think it was a fine choice. As understood by the Reformers and their followers, and by Paul as I read him, this theme is theological, declaring a work of amazing grace; anthropological, demonstrating that we cannot save ourselves; Christological, resting on incarnation and atonement; pneumatological, rooted in Spirit-wrought faith-union with Jesus; ecclesiological, determining both the definition and the health of the Church; eschatological, proclaiming God's truly final verdict on believers here and now; evangelistic, inviting troubled souls into everlasting peace; pastoral, making our identity as forgiven sinners basic to our fellowship; and liturgical, being decisive for interpreting the sacraments and shaping sacramental services. No other biblical doctrine holds together so much that is precious and enlivening. It is a truth that only the humble ever grasp, and it has to be said that despite stirrings of new interest at professional level the modern church tends to fumble it. I recall a passionate lecture some thirty years ago by the late Alan Stibbs, Oak Hill's premier teacher, calling for the reinstatement of the doctrine. Such passion is still, I think, in order.

If these explorations of the biblical, systematic, ecumenical, liturgical and pastoral aspects of the truth of justification commend themselves as in line with Oak Hill's Founder's motto, 'Be right and persist', the authorial team will have its reward.

J. I. PACKER
Regent College
Vancouver, BC

INTRODUCTION

Oak Hill College was founded in 1932 as a theological college of the Church of England. When the silver jubilee approached in 1957 the late Alan Stibbs (Vice-Principal 1937–65 and Senior New Testament Lecturer 1965-71) suggested that the College might publish a staff symposium under the title of 'Biblical Anglicanism'. It was hoped that such a work might be a contribution to the debate which in those days appeared to be shifting the Church of England from its biblical roots.

Nothing came of the suggestion, which was revived with the approach of the golden jubilee in 1982. In view of the ARCIC negotiations it was felt that the subject should be 'Justification by Faith', and each member of the faculty has approached the subject from his own discipline.

The contributors are connected with the College in the following ways:

The Rev Canon Dr James Atkinson was external examiner for the College's DipHE and BA courses from 1976–81. His essay was given in the form of two College Founder's Lectures in December 1980.

The Rev Dr Gerald Bray has been teaching doctrine at Oak Hill College since 1980.

The Rev Michael Butterworth has been teaching Old Testament at Oak Hill College since 1980.

The Rev Canon Dr George Carey taught New Testament at Oak Hill from 1966–70: he is now Principal of Trinity College, Bristol.

The Rev Stephen Motyer was New Testament tutor at Oak Hill College from 1976–83: he is now Rector of Albury with Little Hadham in the diocese of St Albans.

The Rev Dr James Packer began his teaching career at Oak Hill College between undergraduate and post-graduate study in 1948–9: he is now teaching at Regent College, Vancouver, Canada.

The Rev Canon David Wheaton was a tutor at Oak Hill College from 1954 to 1962 and returned as Principal in 1971. His two chapters were originally delivered as part of the Charles Simeon Lectures at Trinity Episcopal School for Ministry at Ambridge, Pennsylvania, in October 1983.

David Field, editor

CONTENTS

1

JUSTIFICATION IN THE OLD TESTAMENT

Mike Butterworth

'Of course one should not write such a work these days' – as Richard Strauss said looking back on his violin concerto. On the one hand, the abstract noun 'justification' finds no place in the Old Testament;[1] on the other, St Paul has already written at some length in our field. However, the question to which Christians have related the term 'justification' from Paul onwards is a central concern of the Old Testament, namely: How does man come to be accepted by God? This question, with its many ramifications, will be the subject of the present essay. Perhaps it will be worth the writing, after all.

Two immediate difficulties arise. The first is that virtually every page of the Old Testament has something to say about the relationship between God and man. Clearly we cannot deal exhaustively with our themes, and we therefore run the risk of making arbitrary selections. We *must* consider Paul's favourite texts on the subject, Genesis 15:6 and Habakkuk 2:4, as well as the Hebrew verb 'to justify'. All of these involve the word 'righteousness' and its derivatives, and it will be convenient to take note of the meaning first. For a consideration of other related terms, e.g. judgment, steadfast love, salvation, which are often found in parallel, we must refer the reader to various standard works.[2]

We still have to decide what else to tackle in the Old Testament, but first let us mention the second problem. This is that we do not always find a direct answer given to our question. We have to ask questions that the biblical writers were not themselves asking or answering, except by implication; so we have to go carefully. The problem is most acute in the case of narrative passages, particularly those in which the narrator takes a low profile. It seems sensible, therefore, to consider narrative passages separately.

The other main subsections proposed, inevitably somewhat arbitrarily, are these: the book of Deuteronomy, which is a clearly defined unit with a great deal to say on our subject; the Pentateuch as a whole, which is agreed by all to be a canonical unit; and the Prophets, with special consideration of Isaiah 40–55, which contains some remarkable teaching, including 53:11 where the verb 'justify' occurs.

This procedure does not imply that there is no profit in considering 'J, E and P' separately. The present writer believes that such an exercise is useful and would confirm a striking similarity and unity between them. For this reason the source to which a passage is assigned is often indicated. This does not, however, imply acceptance of the documentary hypothesis in any of its classical forms.

Righteousness in the Old Testament (ṣedeq, ṣᵉdāqâ)

Back in 1899 H. Cremer,[3] 'with the insight of genius'[4] described 'righteousness' in the Old Testament as a 'concept of relation referring to an actual relationship between two persons and implying behaviour which corresponds to, or is true to, the claims arising out of such a relationship'.[4] This insight has stood the test of time and is probably accepted by the majority of scholars today.[5] In Old Testament theology there is no question of a concept like the Latin *iustitia*, implying an absolute, impersonal standard of justice and righteousness. Still less is there a standard to which both God and man must conform! 'Righteousness' in the Old Testament is based entirely on God's nature. 'You shall be holy for I am holy' illustrates the situation, even though 'holiness' and 'righteousness' are not interchangeable synonyms.

Modern autonomous man is apt to object to this divine monopoly on righteousness, this quality of not being subject to arbitration. The Bible, however, has no such reservations. God has chosen to bring Israel into a relationship with himself. To maintain this relationship both sides must fulfil certain requirements, and to fulfil them is to be righteous. God will check on man's faithfulness and obedience, but man does not need a reciprocal facility: God cannot but act righteously, for he is righteous. (We may want to ask here, 'Which comes first, the righteousness or the acting righteously?' If righteousness *means* fulfilling the demands of a relationship then God can only be righteous in himself if we accept the idea of relationship within the Godhead. Alternatively, we might argue that 'God is righteous' means: he is such that he will always act righteously.)

I would accept this emphasis on relationship, but it is noticeable that where theologies seek to prove that this is the only interpretation, convincing references are hard to come by. Moreover, we should beware of thinking about preserving a relationship in modern terms according to which standards would be entirely pragmatic. The Old Testament writers never lose the sense of fixed norms and standards implied in 'righteousness'. Moreover, they do not always focus their minds on relationships: they are often dealing with particular actions, although these no doubt help or hinder relationships. Thus it is as well to take seriously the type of definition that E. Kautzsch formulated: righteousness is 'a state corresponding to a norm, a norm which remains to be defined in each particular case.'[6]

Attention has been drawn in recent years to the way that 'the poor' and 'the righteous' are equated in the Old Testament. Elizabeth Achtemeier, in a generally excellent article,[7] goes so far as to say, 'Not only is he righteous who fulfils the demands of a relationship, but also he who has his right taken away from him within such a relationship.' This is to overstate the case; the references adduced will not support such a strong statement (e.g. Ps. 103:6 AV, Yahweh works 'righteousness' and 'judgment' for all who are oppressed). The biblical writers invariably have actual oppressed people in mind when they make their statements. 'The poor' is not a sociological term describing those with assets of less than x shekels; it refers to poor people who have other, often undefined, characteristics. It is difficult to imagine a prophet speaking on behalf of a poor man who was significantly more sinful than the rest of society. His poverty would be regarded as a sign of God's displeasure, and he would be called upon to repent. It is also difficult to imagine 'the poor' having much opportunity to sin more grossly than is normal for human beings. Those who have lived among poor people usually find that their very condition makes for closer dependence on and greater receptiveness to God. We cannot say that the poor are righteous *in that* they have been deprived of their right.

However, it is remarkable that 'the righteous' are also recognised to be sinful. Thus Psalm 143 begins: 'Hear my prayer . . . In thy faithfulness answer me, in thy righteousness. Enter not into judgment with thy servant, for *no man* living *is righteous* before thee.' Thus the Psalmist appeals to God's righteousness to ask for salvation for one who is not strictly speaking righteous.

There will be more to say about this when we deal with Genesis 15:6 and Isaiah 40–55. In summary, 'righteousness' describes the way God is and the way he acts; it is particularly used of the requirements of relationships. To be righteous before God means to be accepted by him. 'Righteousness' therefore is a central concern of this essay.

The Verb 'To Justify' (hiṣdîq)

The verb translated 'justify' is derived from the noun ṣedeq, righteousness. It is a causative form[8] and we should expect it to mean 'cause to be righteous', 'make righteous'. A quick check on its occurrences shows that this is generally not the case:

Exod. 23:7   Keep far from a false charge,
           and do not slay the innocent

	and righteous, for I will not justify [RSV, acquit] the wicked.
Deut. 25:1(cf 1Kgs.8:32)	... justifying the just [RSV, acquitting the innocent], and condemning the guilty[9] ...
Prov. 17:15	He who justifies the wicked and he who condemns the righteous are both alike an abomination to the LORD.
Job 27:5	Far be it from me to justify you [RSV, to say that you are right].
Isa. 5:23	[Woe to those] who justify [RSV, acquit] the guilty for a bribe.[10]

The only possible exceptions to this meaning are 2 Samuel 15:4, Psalm 82:3, 'give justice to', Daniel 12:3, 'turn to righteousness' where the meaning does approach a true causative. Isaiah 53:11 is said by some to mean 'make righteous'.

It will be observed that the meaning 'declare righteous' was the normal one over a long period of Israel's history. Daniel 12:3 is the odd man out whether we accept a second- or sixth-century dating. C. R. North uses the extraordinary argument that Daniel 12:3 is 'reminiscent of' Isaiah 53:11 and that 'RV mg "shall make many righteous" has caught the intention of the words.' In Isaiah 50:7 the servant who 'was not rebellious' says 'and I know that I shall not be put to shame; he who justifies [RSV, vindicates] me is near.' This is the closest linguistically to 53:11 and we conclude that *hiṣdîq* means 'declare righteous'. Further discussion of Isaiah 53 is deferred.

Genesis 15:6

'And he [Abraham] believed [in?] the LORD, and he reckoned it to him as righteousness.' The first problem here is to decide what is meant by 'believed'.[11] Both 'believed' and 'believed in/trusted' can be justified etymologically and both find support among eminent scholars. In view of the many differing views expressed, often in detail and with conviction, it seems wise to build a case from the ground floor up. The total number of the verb's occurrences is only fifty and so our conclusions are likely to be tentative.

The clearest meaning of this verb is 'to believe that something is true, or that someone has spoken the truth'. Thus Jacob's 'heart fainted, for he did not believe them', i.e. he did not believe that Joseph was alive and ruling over Egypt (Gen. 45:26). After receiving reassurance he says, 'It is enough; Joseph my son is still alive . . .' (v. 28). In Exodus 4:1, Moses objects, 'they will not believe me or listen to my voice, for they will say, "The LORD did not appear to you"', i.e. they will deny the truth of Moses' claim. Proverbs 14:15 informs us that 'the simple believes everything'.[12]

'Belief that' would seem to be the irreducible minimum in these references, but it is easily seen that something more than mental assent is implied in some – perhaps in all – cases. The word 'trust' could be substituted in place of 'believe', above, and make good sense. Sometimes this 'something more' is passive: an expectation that someone else will act in a certain way or that something will happen. At other times positive action is the inseparable adjunct to the belief. Thus in 1 Samuel 27:12 'Achish trusted David' means he believed that David really was on the Philistines' side against Israel, and allowed him to go on making his raids, presumably without trying to screen him. When the opportunity arose he would take him to battle against Israel.

It is often difficult to decide what nuance the word implies. Several occurrences, particularly where we find a negative, seem on the surface to mean mental assent, but on closer examination are more complicated. E.g. Exodus 4:1 (RSV) reads: '. . . they will not believe me or listen to my voice . . .' and this makes such good sense that we might not question it. However, the phrase 'listen to my voice' usually means 'hearken to', i.e. 'obey me' or at least 'take proper notice of me' as in v. 9 of the same section. In Isaiah 7:9 it seems as though Isaiah simply demands that Ahaz accept his message but, as Wildberger has pointed out, 'believe' occurs on its own (without 'it' following) and other parts of Isaiah make it clear that he expects action and, in fact, inaction: they are *not* to go to Egypt for help and trust in them; they *are* to cleanse themselves and call upon Yahweh.

We conclude that the *hiphil*, *he'emîn*, implies belief in the sense of mental assent and the appropriate positive or negative action as a result of it. Jepsen[13] suggests that the best paraphrases are 'gain stability, rely on someone, give credence to a message or consider it to be true, to trust in someone.' The first of these seems too conjectural for us to accept but the others cover the range of meanings that actually occur.[14]

To decide on the meaning in Genesis 15:16 we must examine the context there. Clearly Abraham *believes* what the Lord says to him – in no case in the Old Testament can we imagine such a notion as 'trust' without 'belief that'. Abraham believes that he will have a son and at first, presumably, that he needs to do nothing except continue normal relations with Sarah. As time goes on it appears that Sarah has no chance of bearing children and she suggests a way in which the promise might still be fulfilled. Abraham responds and Hagar bears his son. Abraham is not rebuked for this action (either in P, 17:15–21, or J, 18:9–15, where Sarah is gently rebuked for her unbelieving laugh). It seems fair to conclude that Abraham's faith basically *consists in* believing the Lord's promise; this commits him to further thinking about what action or inaction is required. In other words *he'emîn* means to believe and not to negate that belief by inappropriate action or inaction.[15]

The most illuminating discussion of the background and meaning of 'faith reckoned as righteousness' is perhaps still that of von Rad.[16] He considers declarations made in the cult, e.g. Leviticus 13:8 'it is leprosy' (cf vv. 17, 25, 28, 37, 44, 46 for different declarations with similar forms), in conjunction with passages like Leviticus 7:18b, '[his sacrifice] shall not be imputed to him', and 17:4, 'blood-guilt shall be imputed to that man'. This indicates that certain authoritative decisions were made and declared by the priest on the basis of appropriate criteria. This declaration was known as 'reckoning' a certain status to an individual. Ezekiel 18:5–9 sets forth criteria for righteousness in a way that is reminiscent of certain cultic passages, and ends with the declaration, 'he is righteous, he shall surely live'. We need not accept the usual assertion that Genesis 15:6 is a late theological comment[17] to see this as the background for vv. 1–6. The criterion used in making the declaration is, however, totally outside the realm of cultic or observable signs. It expresses in the clearest possible way the fact that God accepts a person on the basis of his attitude towards God. It is only possible to disagree with F. Hahn that 'this text comes very close to the Pauline interpretation' on the ground that it actually reaches Paul.[18]

Habakkuk 2:4

Habakkuk's famous verse '. . . the righteous shall live by his faith' came as part of an oracle in answer to two rounds of intense theological questioning with God. The prophet lives among violence and injustice which apparently God does nothing about. The Lord reveals that he is going to bring judgment through the Chaldeans, but this brings the further problem of how the God who is of purer eyes than to behold iniquity can use such an instrument. No doubt Habakkuk also realised that judgment by war is an indiscriminate affair: the innocent seem to perish just as easily as the guilty. The oracle, 2:2ff., suggests delay in the fulfilment of the Lord's purpose but confirms that it will come, and that there will be a difference between the end of the wicked and the righteous: 'Behold, he whose soul is not upright in him shall fail, but the righteous shall live by his faith[fulness]' (Hebrew *'emûnâ*). The oracle continues somewhat obscurely about 'the arrogant man', probably signifying the Chaldeans.

The objection has often been made that Paul misquotes Habakkuk, who does not say anything about faith but speaks only of faithfulness. New Testament scholars are also divided over whether Paul's words mean, 'He who through faith is righteous shall live' (Nygren, Black, Cranfield), or 'The righteous shall live through faith' (Lightfoot, Sanday and Headlam, Leenhardt, Murray).[19] The former would imply a more radical interpretation of Habakkuk, although Nygren still describes this as seeing a deeper significance in the text, in 'entire accord with the exegetical principles then recognised'. We shall be content with discussing what Habakkuk meant and the implication of this for the question of 'justification'.

Habakkuk certainly means that in the time of distress that is coming, those who are faithful to Yahweh will escape or survive. It is impossible here to separate faith from faithfulness. Thus J. B. Lightfoot writes: 'It will thus be seen that 'emûnâ properly represents the passive sense of pistis, as indeed the form of the word shows. But it will at times approach near to the active sense; for constancy under temptation or danger with an Israelite could only spring from reliance on Jehovah'.[20] In such conditions, when even the prophet is forced to ask God what he is doing, faithfulness is not possible without faith; nor is faith worthy of the name if it does not express itself in the activities of faithfulness – although that is more James's problem than Habakkuk's. We might paraphrase Habakkuk's 'emûnâ (faithfulness) as 'active faith'. He is certainly not thinking of simply keeping the Law, but of hanging on to Yahweh's word whatever happens (vv. 2f., especially 3b, 'If it seem slow, wait for it . . .'). The explicit contrast found in Habakkuk is not between law and faith but between the arrogant, self-confident wicked man and the righteous man who places his confidence in Yahweh.

Habakkuk, we must admit, is not primarily speaking of the means by which a person attains the status 'righteous man'. He implies, firstly, that the righteous man will live and, secondly, that the means whereby this comes about is his 'emûnâ. This is as far as he goes.

Narrative Passages

A marvellous feature of most of the narrative of the Old Testament is its restraint. Stories are allowed to flow, and to make their point unobtrusively, without the narrator intervening to point the moral. This quality, however, leaves room for a wide divergence of opinion about details of interpretation.

In approaching the narratives of the Old Testament we are interested primarily in the (canonical) text and its teaching – although this cannot be pursued without due consideration for the authors and editors of the same. We believe, moreover, that the stories are intended as accounts of events that really happened, and that it is legitimate not only to ask about a writer's purpose, but to ask what the significance of the *event* was. We believe there is justification for this approach in the use made of the Scriptures by our Lord in e.g. Luke 4:25–7.

It will be convenient to treat sections separately.

Genesis to Numbers

The so-called primeval history Genesis 1–11 is characterised by increasingly serious accounts of sin and punishment. We are told very clearly how to fall out of fellowship with God: by disobedience, murder, and wickedness (see especially Gen. 3:17; 4:10–12; 6:5). The reason for punishment is less clear in the case of the builders of Babel (Gen. 11:1–9) but is probably pride (vv. 4,6). The story of Cain and Abel is of particular interest and yields some important information despite the obscurity of 4:7. Cain has not 'done well' and is therefore not accepted. The reason is surely not that he has only brought a cereal offering; these were acceptable in the Torah, and it is inconceivable that any Israelite who had a hand in passing on these traditions would have thought such an offering inadequate. The only clue is given in the way the offerings are described: 'of the firstlings . . . and their fat portions' (4:4) on the one hand, and simply 'an offering' on the other. The implication is that Cain's attitude was wrong (cf Mal. 1:6–9).

However, even as he is punished Yahweh continues to converse with him and graciously provides a protective mark (cf the case of Adam and Eve, and their garments of skins).

Noah is described as a 'righteous man, blameless[21] in his generation' who 'walked with God'.[22] The story of the flood tells why and how God decided to destroy all mankind, while continuing to show favour to Noah.[23]

From Genesis 12 onwards we find a constant emphasis on promise and fulfilment. Individual stories make their contribution to this overall theme. We have examined Genesis 15:6 already; it is not just an isolated verse belonging to E or J, or an exilic redactor. It is a comment in and on the final canonical version of the text. Moreover, other parts of the Pentateuchal narrative confirm that Abraham is a man whose life is based on what God has revealed to him. He is blessed because God has chosen him and because Abraham responds in faith (and therefore obedience).[24]

It is remarkable that Abraham is never blessed because of his righteousness. If we wanted to read this into, say, Genesis 13:8f., 14ff., we should have to reckon also with the warts implied in such places as 12:10ff.; 15:3; 16:2 and, especially, 20:2ff. where, notwithstanding the half-truth in Abraham's lie (v. 12), Abimelech is shown to be more righteous.[25]

In Genesis 22:16, 18[26] two reasons are given for God's decision to bless Abraham and multiply his descendants: he has not withheld his only son, and he has obeyed God's voice. We note firstly that this is a decision to confirm a previously made promise; and we observe also the personal way in which God speaks: 'Do not lay your hand on the lad . . . now *I know* that you *fear God* . . . not withheld . . . your only son *from me*' (v. 17). If we may again use the convenient but un-Hebraic word Abraham's attitude has been shown to be right, and that is what God wanted.

When we consider Jacob, his faults are presented with devastating bluntness. I can see no evidence of the writer's revelling in Jacob's trickery of Esau, or Isaac or even Laban, though he does clearly relish the way God thwarts Laban's attempts to cheat Jacob.[27] God first appears to him when he is on the way to Paddan-aram,[28] a journey made necessary by his own deceit. The only evaluative statement in the Jacob–Esau narrative is 'Thus Esau despised his birthright' (Gen. 25:34b). If there is any reason at all therefore for Jacob's blessing it is that he counted the birthright as of major importance. This certainly has more to do with faith than righteousness. The same must be said of Jacob's fight with the angel: he is blessed because he is determined to get a blessing (32:26).

Joseph is portrayed with a minimum of evaluative or theological comment from the narrator (e.g. 50:19f.). His conceit seems to be recognised as such in 37:10 and is the reason for his being sold into Egypt, but that is not said to be a punishment. His righteousness in connection with Potiphar's wife is clearly implied, but is not the reason for his eventual release and rise to power. The emphasis is on God's action: 'But the LORD was with Joseph and showed him steadfast love, and gave him favour in the sight of the keeper of the prison' (39:21). God is the one who reveals the meaning of the various dreams and even Pharaoh recognises this. God is at work behind the scenes bringing his purposes to pass, both punishing sin and bringing salvation to sinful men.[29]

The situation is similar in the case of Moses. No clue is given before Exodus 3[30] that he is especially suitable as a prospective leader. He has a zeal for his own people (2:12), but his rash action does nothing for his authority among them (2:14). When God calls Moses he begins to make excuses; having run out of excuses he says, 'Oh let someone else do it'. As a result of his experiences and his obedience Moses does become a great leader, but we still see him being corrected by God (14:15), receiving advice from his father-in-law, a Midianite priest (18:17ff.), and finally sinning so seriously that he is excluded from going into the promised land (Num. 20:10–12). There has been much disagreement about the nature of Moses' sin: 'Because you did not believe in me, to sanctify me in the eyes of the people of Israel' (v. 12). The most likely explanation is that he does not give all the credit to the Lord, 'shall *we* bring forth water . . .?' (v. 10).[31]

Many other stories contain great interest for our subject.

Thus Balaam, like Moses, is condemned for a sin that is only vaguely specified. On the surface he sounds very pious (Num. 22:18f.), and the story as we have it certainly does not intend to imply that God changes his mind. The most likely explanation is that Balaam, *knowing* the command of the Lord, looks for a way of getting round it (cf 1 Sam. 13:13; 15:19, 22f.; 1 Kgs. 13:17–24).

The story of the bronze serpent (Num. 21:4–9) is suggestive enough for Jesus to have used it as a picture of himself on the cross, according to John 3:14. The people who were bitten by snakes had simply to look at the bronze snake and live. It is difficult to imagine a clearer picture of salvation coming to sinful men under judgment simply by God's mercy through faith.

Other Passages

Mere outlines must suffice now, for time would fail me to tell of Joshua, Ehud, Gideon, and the rest. The general conclusions drawn from the narrative already examined are strengthened, whether we look to Judges, or Samuel, or Kings, or Isaiah or Jeremiah. The Lord is the prime mover; no reason is offered why he should choose to bring certain people into a relationship with himself. Indeed, we cannot say that he would not be more inclined to choose a person who showed good qualities,[32] but several times the weakness and unsuitableness of his choice is emphasised. Thus Barak will not even go to battle unless Deborah goes with him, the battle 'will not lead to his glory for the LORD will sell Sisera into the hand of a woman.'[33] Gideon is the least member of the lowliest clan in Manasseh, afraid of the men of the city and even his own family, a man who needs a special and repeated sign before he will act; the key to his success is simply that the Lord is with him,[34] and so it is that he delivers Israel with a mere 300 men.[35] Samson, for all his physical strength and uproarious exploits, achieves more as a weak man, degraded because of his sin, than he did during the rest of his life.[36]

Some hints are given in the narratives concerning the choice of Samuel, Saul and David. Samuel is chosen while still a boy; Saul is from the least family in the least tribe, although he is taller than anyone else![37] David is ruddy with beautiful eyes, but is not even considered a possibility by his father, nor by other men presumably, since 'the LORD looks not on the outward appearance but on the heart' (1 Sam. 16:7). This last phrase is reminiscent of 1 Samuel 13:14 (NIV) 'the LORD has sought out a man after his own heart'.[38]

We have seen that obedience is necessary for the relationship with God to continue. Saul is rejected because he applied a little imagination to the prophet's instruction from the Lord – despite the fact that afterwards he repents.[39] David's adultery and murder, on the other hand, do not lead to David's disqualification, although the thing that he has done 'displeases the LORD' and the child born to Bathsheba dies, and the sword does not depart from David's house. We cannot doubt that the editorial comment of Kings expresses the matter accurately, 'his heart was wholly true to the LORD . . . all the days of his life.'[40]

The wealth of material is again overwhelming. Let us be content to mention Naaman, the Syrian general, worshipper of Rimmon. He believes the word of God through the prophet – enough to humble himself and obey. And his leprosy is taken away.

Throughout these examples we have assumed that God's dealings with individuals in concrete historical situations give a true picture of their relationship (we might even say spiritual relationship) with God. As Manoah's wife might have said, 'If the Lord had not intended to save us, would he have done all these things.' We may leave a detailed justification of their typological significance to the men of the New Testament and after.[41] Suffice it for our purposes to view them simply as flesh-and-blood human beings whom God favoured and blessed.

Deuteronomy

Deuteronomy provides the clearest formulations of how and why Israel came to be God's people. The important annual confession of 26:5–11 sets out the main events and hints at the reasons for them: '... cried to the LORD, the God of our fathers', and 'the LORD heard ... saw our affliction, our toil, and our oppression'. The people threw themselves on to the mercy of the Lord. The continuity of the covenant relationship established through Moses is emphasised, and linked with God's compassion.

The rest of the book underlines and develops the same themes. Yahweh, the only God, Lord of heaven and earth, has chosen Israel to be his unique and exclusive possession. Why Israel? That is a mystery; it is not because of any special merit; neither her numbers nor her righteousness would have qualified her for special treatment (7:7; 9:4–6). Other nations are sometimes singled out for judgment because of their exceptional wickedness, but stiff-necked Israel is often just as bad.[42]

So clearly is this expressed in Deuteronomy that we are able to put to the book directly the question, 'How can sinful man come into a relationship with God?' We may be sure that had the writer spoken Reformation English he might well have answered, 'solely through God's electing grace'. This is not meant to imply that the Reformation overtones to these words are all present in Deuteronomy, but the basic concept of God's loving, saving initiative is undoubtedly the same.

We must ask what place 'righteousness' and '*tôrâ*' (law) have in Deuteronomy, for the book stresses frequently and emphatically the need to keep God's statutes and ordinances. This passage (4:5–8) catches the writer's general attitude to the Law:

> Behold I have taught you statutes and ordinances, as the LORD my God commanded me, that you should do them in the land which you are entering to take possession of it. Keep them and do them; for that will be your wisdom and your understanding in the sight of the peoples, who, when

they hear all these statutes, will say, 'Surely this great nation is a wise and understanding people.' For what great nation is there that has a god so near to it as the LORD our God is to us, whenever we call upon him? And what great nation is there that has statutes and ordinances so righteous as all this law which I set before you this day?

It is a privilege for Israel to have this law to guide them in practical matters and into deeper understanding of the Lord. It belongs with the blessing of the deliverance from oppression in Egypt and the inheritance of the land of Canaan, and is their natural consequence. We can imagine the writer's being just as flabbergasted as Paul at the question, 'Why not do evil that good may come?'[43] God has called the people to belong to him and that implies that they must be one with him in purpose: they must be absolutely loyal to the Lord and determined to follow his direction – his *tôrâ*. That is why idolatry is emphasised as *the* sin which will separate them from him, and cause the covenant to be broken. That is also why restoration after sin comes through repentance, a whole-hearted turning back to the Lord. This is most graphically and powerfully expressed in 4:29. Even when they go astray and end up serving idols in foreign lands, idolaters will find God again if they search with all their heart.[44]

Deuteronomy proclaims a strong doctrine of rewards and punishments based on the people's faithfulness. Careful obedience to the Law will bring prosperity in every way: they will take possession of the land (8:1, etc.), their crops and animals will flourish and increase (7:12–14), the poor will become at least middle class (15:4f.), and even disease will vanish (7:15). Disobedience, by contrast, will in the first place bring corrective chastening; the Lord continues to love his erring people, and will seek to bring them back to himself. If, however, they deliberately persist in rebelling, they will be in danger of being cut off. All of this is to be seen within the context of the covenant. None of it weakens the force of 9:6, '. . . God is not giving you this good land to possess because of your righteousness'.

It is surprising that Paul did not make more use of Deuteronomy's theology. He takes his quotations mainly from the
laws themselves. Here it is necessary to say something about
27:26 which is quoted in Galatians 3:10 as a statement of what
justification by the Law means and how it operates: if a man
does not keep everything perfectly he is under a curse.
Obviously the Israelites would not be thinking in terms of
perfect, absolute righteousness when they used this liturgy
('commination service'). Paul implies however that the words
can be pressed so as to refer to this and remain true. Whether
the authority for this understanding of the text is Deuteronomy's or Paul's is thus debatable, but we have seen that there is in
any case some warrant for saying that Old Testament writers
may have been aware of two levels of speaking and thinking at
this point. Job, for instance, insists that he is blameless and
upright and God confirms this. Yet Job also acknowledges that
one cannot be absolutely righteous before God.[45]

The Pentateuch

It is time to draw together the various threads considered in the
Pentateuch. The picture that emerges is consistent. God desires
to redeem sinful man and *he* initiates any significant action to
this end. He brings individuals into fellowship with himself
despite their unfitness. 'Righteousness' is naturally not
irrelevant and sometimes refers to keeping the Law; at the
same time, however, righteousness implies commitment to a
relationship with Yahweh. Thus what Paul (at least) means by
faith expresses fairly closely what God looks for according to
the Pentateuch; and this would apply also to the other parts of
the Old Testament that we have touched upon.

Other features of the Pentateuch confirm these conclusions:
the covenants with Noah, Abraham, Moses (and, later,
David), the theme of promise – fulfilment which overarches
the whole, the way that the Law is firmly set in the covenant
context. We have no space to enlarge on these matters, but
must mention one particular problem.

Leviticus 18:5 is quoted by Paul[46] to illustrate the principle
of justification by works which he is so much against. This was
not the original intention of the passage. The reference to the
deliverance from Egypt (v.3) and to Yahweh's bringing the
people to the land of Canaan imply that the deliverance from
Egypt is the basis on which the command is given. The promise
of life is therefore given to a people who have already been
given life. The passage is, in fact, consonant with the pattern
found in various forms in both Old and New Testaments:
God's choice of and blessing to his people; their response of
thankfulness and continuing obedience. Why, then, does Paul
seem to repudiate the direct meaning of this Old Testament
passage? It is because he is considering law on its own and
pressing the meaning of 18:5 beyond its original intention (cf
Deut. 27:26 above). Again, the point for us to note is that it
remains true even when pressed. We may put it this way: 'Do
the law and you will live!' is true in an absolute sense. The Law
of God would provide a way of justification – if only someone
could comply perfectly with all its demands. As we are,
however, we can be justified only by God's grace. This does
not, of course, remove the need for the justified to keep God's
Law (as Paul recognises in his many exhortations to holy
living). It is a case of 'Continue to do this and you will continue
in life.'

Finally we must mention that the sacrificial system of Israel
pointed to the anomaly that is apparent in the fact of fellowship between the holy God and sinful man. We think particularly of the Day of Atonement ritual (Lev. 16), the curtain of
the tabernacle (e.g. 21:23), and the various regulations regarding uncleanness. If a full answer to the anomaly is not given in
the Pentateuch it is at least evident that sin as such is an
obstacle to this fellowship and therefore must be dealt with
(including sin done in ignorance), and that God is the one who
must take the initiative in doing this.

The Prophets

There is significant material throughout the prophetic books: Habakkuk 2:4 has been mentioned; Isaiah acknowledges himself to be 'a man of unclean lips' and is cleansed (in his vision) by a coal from the altar; Jeremiah speaks much of repentance, turning away from sin and returning to the Lord, including the possibility of avoiding judgment and the point beyond which this is impossible; and his own sufferings, with his so-called 'confessions', prepare us to understand the vision of vicarious suffering which we find in Isaiah 53. We may also think of Ezekiel's prophecies of restoration, including the new Temple; or of the love of God emphasised in Hosea. It seems best, however, to concentrate in these closing paragraphs on the teaching of Isaiah 40–55 where we discover something quite distinctive and, in chapter 53, unique.

In these chapters God's righteousness becomes almost synonymous with his salvation. Thus, in chapter 45 the words 'righteous', 'righteousness' occur seven times in connection with the deliverance of Israel from Babylon through Cyrus. It is 'righteous' for God to save sinful Israel. Chapter 46:12–13 is especially notable:

> Hearken to me you *stubborn of heart*
> you who are far from *righteousness* [RSV deliverance]
> I bring near my *righteousness* [RSV deliverance], it is not far off
> and my *salvation* will not tarry;
> I will put *salvation* in Zion
> for Israel my glory.

The climax is in 53:11:

> . . . by his knowledge shall the *righteous* one, my servant, make many to be *accounted righteous*;
> and he shall bear their iniquities.

Many attempts have been made to refute the interpretation that this text refers to vicarious suffering. Thus R. N.

Whybray[47] refers to Lamentations 5:7 to argue that to bear another's sin means to bear the consequences of another's sinful deeds. The method he employs throughout Isaiah 53 is to ambush particular phrases and expressions and to persuade them one by one that they fit his own theory that 'the servant' is the prophet himself, giving thanks after being liberated from a Babylonian prison. To make their case he and others resort to various textual emendations which find little support from the ancient versions nor even from one another's. The only safe course is to take the text as it stands, with all its difficulties, unless it is impossible to make sense of it;[48] and this we now do.

In seeking to understand what Isaiah 52:13–53:12 is saying we note that:

1. The Lord has some special purpose in the suffering of the Servant; it is not merely an unfortunate consequence of other people's sin.

2. The suffering is described in many ways:

   He is despised, esteemed as nothing.

   He is oppressed and afflicted, cut off out of the land of the living; he pours out his soul to death, is buried with the wicked and 'a rich man'.

   He is numbered with transgressors.

   He bears our griefs (pains?) and sorrows (sicknesses?), iniquities and sin.

   He is made (or makes himself) a guilt offering.

   He is wounded, bruised, stricken because of transgression and iniquities.

   He has laid upon him the 'chastisement of our peace (or wholeness)' and the iniquity of us all.

   The passage thus gives a central place to describing this suffering, showing both its nature and its purpose.

3. The result of this suffering is that:

   He sees his offspring, prolongs his days, divides spoil with the great, affects kings and nations, sees the fruit of his labours, prospers the will of the Lord;

   we are made whole, healed and justified. Something more is intended here than sharing in the results of defeat in war or pestilence or any of the traditional judgments of the Old Testament; there is more spoken of than the incidental suffering of a prophet like Jeremiah or the pain of intercession. What the Lord refused to do through the great intercessor, his servant Moses (Exod. 32:32f.), he does through that greater intercessor, the servant of the Lord.

It is true that this vision is unique in the Old Testament. Yet it is not without points of contact. The sacrificial system points to death as the means whereby sin is removed and man stands 'righteous' before God. The reference to guilt offering (Isa. 53:10) surely draws attention to this. There are hints of the same sort of thinking in Zechariah 9–14[49] (another favourite source of inspiration for Jesus). So we have no hesitation in affirming that this passage does teach the justification of the ungodly through vicarious suffering (which includes death in fact). The need for faith or trust is not evident here; nor is it emphasised in Isaiah 40–55 – but it does seem to be assumed in such expressions as 'they shall understand' (52:15) and the form of the confession in 53:4–6, etc., with acknowledgment of a lack of understanding previously (cf many other expressions in Isa. 40–55 especially 50:10; 55:1, 6f.).

Summary

The present writer is aware how inadequate and incomplete this essay is, and can only appeal to the reader to check that what is said here does give a fair reflection of the Old Testament's teaching on the subject of 'justification'. The following seems to represent the sort of conclusions that might be drawn on the assumption that one could ask the question 'How does a person come to be accepted by God?' of the Old Testament, and without considering the New Testament.

No one is fit to come into a relationship with God and all without exception must depend on his grace whereby he takes the initiative. Why he chooses particular persons or nations cannot be guessed, but in fact he did choose Israel through

Abraham, with the purpose that his salvation might extend to the farthest places of the world. He accepts those who hear a message as from him and respond in faith and obedience. The response involves 'belief that . . .' but not in the sense of merely believing doctrines or propositions; rather it means believing what *God* reveals *because* it is God that reveals it. Obedience is inseparable from this belief or faith. Several different expressions emphasise the personal nature of the response that God requires: trust, fear, hearken to the voice of, serve, etc.

God himself must also deal with sin since it is a constant barrier between men and himself. Mere repentance and forgiveness are not possible; the system of cultic ordinances and, above all, the picture of the suffering Servant show that God does deal with sin without compromising his own revealed standards. In some mysterious way the punishment of our sin is borne by another who thus justifies many.

'What shall I render to the LORD for all his bounty to me? I will lift up the cup of salvation and call on the name of the LORD' (Ps. 116:12–13).

2

RIGHTEOUSNESS BY FAITH IN THE NEW TESTAMENT

Steve Motyer

> Because all men be sinners and offenders against God, and
> breakers of his law and commandments, therefore can no
> man, by his own acts, works, and deeds, seem they never so
> good, be justified and made righteous before God: but every
> man, of necessity, is constrained to seek for another right-
> eousness or justification, to be received at God's own hands.

Thus begins the famous *Homily on Salvation* which forms part
of the dogmatic foundation of the Anglican church.[1] Two
things strike the modern reader immediately: we see the
concern of the Reformers (in this case, of Archbishop Cranmer
himself) to ground their authoritative dogmatic pronounce-
ments in the Bible, so that we discern here allusions to Romans
3:20, 23; Galatians 2:16; Isaiah 64:6; and Philippians 3:9;
and we notice how the theme of 'justification' was understood
as central to 'salvation' – a view reflected repeatedly in this
Homily. The Reformers, who thus sought to put into practice
their understanding of the Church as *semper reformanda*,
always subject to the scrutiny of the word of God in order
constantly to be reshaped by it, would have been the first to
agree that this process of gathering and synthesising verses into
dogmatic statements could be dangerous: that it runs the risk
of altering the original harmonisation of the Scriptural
melody, or even of unintentionally changing the tune

altogether. They would encourage us to the task that lies before us in this paper – to seek to hear Scripture speak again in its own tones, sitting light as we do so to all our inherited understanding, which without the music of the Word will in any case become rigid and lifeless.

Two preliminary observations set the scene. The first is that, as such, there is *no* doctrine of justification in the New Testament: rather, there is a doctrine of *righteousness*. 'Justification', or 'justify', are words chosen by English translators to render some members of a group of Greek words all beginning with the stem *dikai-*, most usually the verb *dikaioō*; but other members of the same group, for instance the noun *dikaiosunē* or the adjective *dikaios*, are regularly translated 'righteousness', 'righteous', and this is undoubtedly the more accurate translation. The trouble is that in modern English there is no verb in the 'right-' word-group: 'rightify' does not exist. Some scholars have suggested that the old English verb 'rightwise' should be resurrected as a substitute for 'justify'; but it seems best to keep the traditional 'justify', while bearing in mind that the distinction which this introduces between the verb *dikaioō* and the rest of the word-group does not represent a distinction within the word-group itself.

Secondly, we observe the distribution and use of *dikai-* in the New Testament. We are immediately struck by the fact that, although the Reformers, and many others, have felt that 'justification' summarises the Gospel, yet it is by no means a constant theme of the New Testament. In fact, it is only in Paul (total occurrence of root: 113 times) that it can be said to be prominent, but even here it is not *constant*: Galatians (13) and Romans (63) are occupied with it, but the Thessalonian letters (3) and the massive Corinthian correspondence (11) get by largely without it. Among the Evangelists, only Matthew (26) and Luke (19) make anything of 'righteousness'. Statistics can of course deceive, but the immediate impression one receives is that 'righteousness' was regarded by Paul as a central Gospel theme *when he considered the application of the Gospel to certain pressing problems*, tackled particularly in Romans and Galatians. The implication of this might be that Paul, or any

New Testament author, if asked to state the Gospel dogmatically in the way attempted by Archbishop Cranmer in the *Homily on Salvation*, would not immediately use the *dikai-*word-group as the indispensable core of a reply. They might in fact feel that the Gospel can fully be stated only in a *missionary* setting, and that there were and are missionary situations in which 'justification' would be an inappropriate theme to present as the heart of the Gospel. We are going to need a very delicate exegetical touch as we try to discover how exactly justification was understood in the New Testament Church, so as to test our own view of the Gospel we are committed to proclaim.

Righteousness in Matthew

We begin with Matthew. He is marked off from the other evangelists particularly by his use of the noun *dikaiosunē* (righteousness), which appears seven times in all, including five in the Sermon on the Mount (5:6, 10, 20; 6:1, 33; elsewhere, 3:15 and 21:32). The verb *dikaioō* appears twice and the adjective *dikaios* 17 or 18 times.[2] He carefully builds on the usage of the Old Testament and of his contemporaries, as Benno Przybylski has shown.[3] In the Old Testament, the heart of the meaning of 'righteousness' is *that which is well-pleasing to God, which receives approval in the heavenly court.* And because God has revealed himself as one who cares for outcasts, and who seeks to bring a people into communion with himself by great acts of salvation, the 'righteousness' pleasing to him has a distinctive character. He himself expresses it not by condemning sinners, but by saving them: one is hard put to it to find more than a couple of places where his righteousness implies or is even associated with exacting punishment as judge. This is hard for us to grasp, used as we are to think of 'righteousness' in terms of *distributive justice*, as the principle which guarantees absolute fairness, so that each receives as nearly as possible what he deserves. This is not the connotation of righteousness in the Old Testament, where 'the righteousnesses of the Lord' (Judg. 5:11) are his mighty acts of salvation on behalf of a people who were thereby the recipients of a completely *undeserved* mercy. When this God demands of his elected and saved people a righteousness conforming to his own character, we are not surprised to find that it is one which likewise steps in on behalf of the outcast and the sinners, because at its heart lies worship and love of the God who has done just that for Israel. This explains Matthew's extraordinary (to us) statement about Joseph's response to his discovery of Mary's pregnancy, where the fact of Joseph's *righteousness* is mentioned to explain the *leniency* and *mercy* of his plans for his apparently wayward fiancée (1:19 NIV). It also illuminates the two uses of *dikaiosunē* outside the Sermon on the Mount, which balance and supplement each other: 'John came to you in the way of righteousness', says Jesus (21:32), referring not just to the personal righteousness of John's life but rather to the righteous purpose of God which had appointed him, like all the prophets, to 'turn many of the sons of Israel to the Lord their God' (Luke 1:16); and this is the same saving righteousness which Jesus then 'fulfils', taking over God's purpose of salvation from his great forerunner (Matt. 3:15).[4]

Turning to the Sermon on the Mount, we are struck by the way in which Matthew does not distinguish between God's righteousness and man's. 'Seek first his kingdom and his righteousness' (6:33) probably does not refer primarily to the ethical righteousness which Jesus' disciples must seek to attain, but (in parallel to 'kingdom') to the eschatological completion of God's purpose of salvation, for which we yearn. If that is correct, then this will be the meaning of 'Blessed are those who hunger and thirst for righteousness' (5:6) also. But it would be wrong to deny that in both these verses the thought is of *righteousness resting upon man*, for the longing expressed in 5:6 is to be *caught up* in God's saving purpose. Then 5:20 makes it clear that this places a rigorous ethical demand on us, 'unless your righteousness exceeds that of the scribes and Pharisees, you will never enter the Kingdom of heaven', and 6:1 NIV speaks simply of 'your acts of righteousness'. This ethical meaning fits in with Matthew's overall emphasis on the call to discipleship, and is always in mind when he uses the adjective *dikaios*.

But how is it possible for two such different meanings – God's saving purpose and the righteousness man himself must attain – to sit side by side with no apparent sense of inconsistency? The problem is clearly posed when we look at 25:31–46, the 'parable' of the sheep and the goats, to which Matthew gives a position of great structural importance in his Gospel as he directs our eyes forward to the climax of God's purposes at the end. There the righteous, although they 'inherit the kingdom prepared for you from the foundation of the world' (25:34), nonetheless do so on the basis of their own works of righteousness performed in this life: 'for I was hungry and you gave me food . . .' (25:35). It will not do simply to interpret the righteous as 'the justified'. Matthew is certainly picturing for us the ultimate fulfilment of God's saving righteousness to which Jesus looks forward in 3:15; but even if 'the righteous' in 25:37, 46 has this overtone, the basically ethical, achievement-related force of the title cannot be denied. It is not just that Matthew seems to contradict Paul's insistence that we cannot be justified on the basis of our own works (Rom. 3:20, etc.), but also that there seems to be a great tension within his own Gospel.

This problem is best tackled from Paul's side. But before we turn to him, we must note that Matthew is again faithfully reflecting the Old Testament tradition in which he was brought up and which he was anxious to reconcile with Christian faith. We encounter precisely the same tension, for instance, in the Psalms, where on the one hand tremendous confidence is expressed in the capacity of men to be righteous before God (e.g. 34:15; 52:6; 58:10–11) – so much so that appeal is sometimes made to God on the basis of the Psalmist's own righteousness (e.g. 7:8; 18:20–4; 26:1) – but on the other hand there is a realistic awareness that 'no man living is righteous before thee' (143:2), that men were conceived in sin (51:5), and that therefore the only sure hope is the mercy and 'righteousness' of God (e.g. 31:1; 71:2–5; 130). The extra-

ordinary thing is that these two views exist side by side, in
Matthew as in the Old Testament, with no sense of tension.
Matthew must have moved in a biblical and theological
thought-world which held them together as natural bedfellows
– but how? It was Paul to whom it fell to wrestle with this
problem because, as we shall see, it is bound up with the whole
issue of his apostleship to the Gentiles, and was therefore
something with which he had to deal as he sought to give a
biblical and theological justification for his call. To Paul,
therefore, we now turn.

Paul in Debate at Antioch

It is hard for us to imagine and understand the suspicion with
which Paul's missionary activities were viewed by some other
parts of the Church. Luke records that 'a vast host' (Acts
21:20) of Jewish Christians in Jerusalem were not prepared to
extend a welcome to him when he arrived with a gift for them
from the Gentile churches. Paul had set out on this visit with
trepidation, hoping that the gift would be a means of demonstrating a unity in the church which was far from obvious
(Rom. 15:25–32). What was the reason for this suspicion
which threatened to divide the Church? Luke gives it as the
rumour that Paul was teaching Jews to abandon the Mosaic
law (Acts 21:21). In fact Paul did no such thing: we see from
Romans 14 that he encouraged Jewish Christians to maintain
their observance of 'the customs', and criticised those who
passed judgment on them for so doing. But something must
have given rise to this exaggeration. Perhaps the incident at
Antioch which Paul himself records (Gal. 2:11ff.) had contributed to his bad reputation in Jerusalem, for it was
sparked off by the arrival of a deputation from there, who
doubtless took back news of Paul's deeply suspect attitude. We
must look carefully at this important passage, for it lies at the
heart of Paul's teaching about righteousness.

The Church at Antioch was a mixed fellowship of Jewish
and Gentile Christians – in fact, according to Acts 11:19–26,

the first such Church to exist. This meant that Jews and Gentiles ate together – indeed, did so as the central act of their worship, for the Lord's Supper was celebrated as a common meal. But this meant also the abandoning of a deeply-felt Jewish scruple: to eat with Gentiles was to run the risk of breaking the food laws, either through the food itself or through the vessels used to prepare and serve the meal, and was strongly forbidden. No wonder the Jerusalem Church sent an observer, to see exactly what was happening (Acts 11:22). Paul had already been a member of this church for a long time 'when Cephas came to Antioch' (Gal. 2:11), and he regarded it as his spiritual home (Acts 11:25f.; 13:1–3; 14:26–8 etc.). Peter at first fitted in with the local custom (Gal. 2:12), perhaps remembering his experience with Cornelius, when he himself had been persuaded to quell his natural feelings and engage in table-fellowship with Gentiles (Acts 10), or perhaps (if this Antioch incident is to be dated after Acts 15:1–35) hoping that the compliance of the Antiochene Church with the apostolic decree about Gentiles and the law (Acts 15:23–9) would make it possible for him to join in without offending the Jerusalem believers. But then 'certain men came from James' and persuaded him to withdraw (Gal. 2:12); and following his example all the Jewish members of the Antiochene Church, including Barnabas the original Jerusalem 'observer', who had never previously had problems about the common meal, broke away and set up a separate fellowship.

Who were these men from James, and with what arguments did they urge this split? They were plainly members of or associated with 'the circumcision party' (Gal. 2:12), whom we encounter in Acts 11:2 and 15:1. We cannot assume that they rightly represented James' point of view (cf Acts 15:24), though they plainly appealed to his authority, and were felt by Paul to have been in some sense authorised by him. At any rate, we may fairly reconstruct their arguments as follows:

1. The whole Christian Church is getting the reputation among Jews of sitting light to the law, because of your lax behaviour. This is making missionary activity more difficult.
2. Standard synagogue missionary practice offers an

appropriate model for the Church. Gentiles are welcomed as worshippers, but are not admitted to table-fellowship until they become Jewish proselytes. You should do the same.

3. In fact a vital theological principle is at stake here. Who are the people of God? Israel alone is the elect people to whom that title can be applied, and the coming of the Messiah does not affect the principle that if one wishes to enter the covenant of grace, he must become a member of Israel. The God-given means of such entry is circumcision.

4. Obedience to the law by the Gentiles is therefore a matter not just of missionary convenience, but also of theological necessity. God does not go back on or rescind his word. His law is a gift to all men, not just to the Jews, and acceptance of Jesus as the Christ makes no difference to that.

The power of this argument lay in its simplicity. It is not surprising that the Jewish Christians in Antioch were swayed. There is no evidence that Peter accepted points 3 and 4, and in any case it is possible that the men from James majored on points 1 and 2. The other two were argued strongly by the 'circumcision party', and the influence of this powerful lobby was plainly felt keenly by Peter (Gal. 2:12), even though the evidence indicates that he and James were not members. Its influence reached as far as the new churches in Galatia, founded on Antiochene principles through a mission launched from there, and the acceptance of points 3 and 4 by some of the Galatian Christians prompted Paul's fiery letter, including his report of the 'Antioch incident'. For he clearly saw that 3 and 4 are the theological foundation which alone would give weight, if correct, to the first two arguments – and that giving way in the face of arguments 1 and 2, as Peter had done, was tantamount to conceding the whole position of the 'circumcision party'. Hence the 'insincerity' of Peter's action (Gal. 2:13). For Paul, on the other hand, the Antiochene table-fellowship between Jews and Gentiles was not a mere concession to the natural reluctance of Gentile Christians to adopt strange Jewish customs, but a matter of principle which arose from the heart of the Gospel which Christ had called him to preach to the Gentiles. Galatians is Paul's fiery exposition of this Gospel in direct relation to the threat to his Gentile converts posed by the 'circumcision party'. Later, Romans takes up the same issues in greater depth, to help especially the Jewish Christians in Rome wrestling with the problem of their own identity in Christ. And at the heart of this Gospel which Paul expounds lies the theme of righteousness.

Paul's Argument to the Galatians

Galatians 2:14b–21 probably summarises what Paul said to Peter when he opposed him to his face; it certainly says in a nutshell what the whole of Galatians seeks to argue. Verses 15–16 could hardly be more emphatic:

> We ourselves, who are Jews by birth and not Gentile sinners, yet who know that a man is not justified by works of the law but through faith in Jesus Christ, even we have believed in Christ Jesus, in order to be justified by faith in Christ, and not by works of the law, because by works of the law shall no one be justified.

This marvellous sentence is a chiasmus balanced around the main clause, 'even we have believed in Christ Jesus'; and, interestingly, the last clause echoes the language of Psalm 143:2, which we quoted earlier. Paul is moving in the same thought-world as Matthew. Within the chiastic structure, this last clause balances the first, 'We ourselves, who are Jews by birth and not Gentile sinners', so that 'Jews by birth' and 'works of the law' correspond to each other. This correspondence would be warmly affirmed by Paul's opponents (cf arguments 3 and 4 above), who regarded their Jewish descent and their possession of the law as parallel and priceless privileges: what greater blessing could be imagined than membership of the elect people of God, chosen by God from the nations for his own, and given the law both as a sign of this uniqueness and as his guide to the enjoyment of the life with himself, into which he had so graciously brought them?[5] For these Jewish Chris-

tians the final proof of God's goodwill towards Israel was to be
seen in his gift of the Messiah according to his promise. We can
sense the strength of their outrage when we see that Paul, on
the other hand, engages in a polemic against these two priceless gifts. He (like Peter) had come to see that, though a Jew, he
must 'live [i.e. find spiritual life] *as a Gentile*' (Gal. 2:14); and
he was now absolutely convinced that 'works of the law' were
not capable of effecting or preserving acceptance with God the
judge within the covenant. Paul's opponents regarded him as,
in effect, believing that Christ was an 'agent of sin' (Gal. 2:17),
because according to Paul Christ summons Jews to abandon
the law and become 'Gentile sinners' – this phrase in Galatians
2:15 reflects the belief that because the Gentiles do not have
the law to guide them, they must by definition be sinners. The
accusation against Paul quoted in Romans 3:8 – that he taught
'why not do evil that good may come?' – is closely related.

Indeed, reading Galatians 2:15–16, it is hard to resist the
conclusion that Paul wishes to drop the Old Testament, and to
regard it and Israel as having been abrogated by God through
Christ, so that now the people of God exist on entirely new
terms. This is certainly what Marcion, one of Paul's most
ardent admirers in the second century, thought he had taught.
But it is hard to reconcile this interpretation of Paul with the
fact that he constantly quotes the Old Testament as pointing
forward to Christ, and wrestles, not to write off his heritage,
but (like Matthew) to reconcile it with his Christian faith.
Marcion could only carry through this interpretation by
'bowdlerising' Paul, removing the many places where he expresses a positive view of the law, or of Israel. Many scholars
today conclude that Paul was simply muddled; that in essence
Marcion was right, in that he discerned what Paul felt in his
heart of hearts but never managed consistently to state; and
that in fact Peter was not the only one who was pressurised
into inconsistency by the 'circumcision party'. Is this correct?
This whole area of Pauline theology is much disputed, but it
seems to me to be possible to show Paul's position to have been
much more integrated and consistent than this – as indeed the
later Church instinctively saw, in that it condemned Marcion

as a heretic but did not on the other hand accept the position of Paul's opponents, thus naturally adopting a middle position.

Paul's own exposition of Galatians 2:15–16 follows immediately in verses 17–21 – and then in the rest of Galatians and Romans! He makes four points in Galatians 2:17–21 which form the heart of his thinking:

1. 'I *through the law* died to the law, that I might live to God' (v. 19). Paul suggests, remarkably, that the law itself told him to look elsewhere for life.
2. 'I do not nullify the grace of God; for if *dikaiosunē* [RSV: justification] were through the law, then Christ died to no purpose' (v. 21). Paul was accused of setting God's grace at nought by rejecting his precious gift of the law. He counters by pointing out sharply that his opponents, with their exceedingly high view of the law, can have no theology of the cross. If God's grace has been exhausted in the election of Israel and the gift of the law, the death of his Messiah is just an embarrassment to be explained away.
3. 'I have been crucified with Christ; it is no longer I who live, but Christ who lives in me . . .' (v. 20). The death of the Christ, rather than being an embarrassment, forms for Paul the heart of his experience of spiritual life, through union or identification with him who is now risen.
4. '. . . and the life I now live in the flesh I live by faith in the Son of God' (v. 20). Paul reiterates that 'faith', so emphasised in verse 16, is the basis of new life in the Messiah.

These four points we shall now examine in the light of Paul's writings elsewhere. But first it is necessary to ask ourselves what the significance is of the first person singular to which he switches in Galatians 2:18–21. It would be easy for us to pass over it as simply the language of personal confession – which would not be a false judgment, but would miss an important dimension of it. Paul uses such a first person elsewhere, in the famous section Romans 7:7–8:4, in which he is also concerned with the right understanding of the law. It is the almost universal opinion of scholars that the 'I' of Romans 7 is not solely autobiographical, but that Paul is making himself typical of a group in whose name he speaks.[6] The literary background for such an 'I' is to be found in the Psalms, and particularly in the use of 'I' – Psalms in public worship, universalising the experience of the original Psalmist, who was in any case usually not historically identifiable. Here in Galatians 2 Paul speaks as an archetypal 'Jew by birth' who has found his Messiah (Christ is named eight times in these seven verses), and thus traces in his own person the path which Israel must follow: not just Paul but Israel as a whole must die to the law and be crucified with Christ so that the Messiah may now 'live' in Israel spiritually, just as he once did physically.

These four points are all much disputed in the scholarly world. Since there is insufficient space to debate each point with reference to the work of other scholars, I simply ask the reader to judge for himself whether the following interpretation of Paul holds water or not.

1 The Law

Contrary to the view of several scholars, Paul never felt compelled by his Christian faith to dispute the divine *origin* of the Law; rather, he sought to clarify the *purpose* and *limitations* of the Law, in the light both of the Old Testament itself and of the coming of the Christ. He develops his remarkable 'through the law' (Gal. 2:19) in several ways in Galatians 3.

(a) All that the law offers is a precarious existence 'under a curse'. This phrase in Galatians 3:10 is not the equivalent of 'cursed', for Paul is thinking of the legal framework of life which Israel took upon herself when she affirmed the law, upon entry into the promised land, using the liturgy recorded in Deuteronomy 27:11–26. It was a framework in which she stood 'under' both a blessing and a curse, but chiefly under the latter, for at any moment her disobedience to the Law could bring in train the actual curses listed in such awful detail (much more so than the blessings) in chapter 28, and there is a sneaking feeling – expressed explicitly at 31:16, 29 – that experience of the curse is absolutely inevitable, because 'to this day the Lord has not given you a mind to understand . . .'

(29:4), and he has not yet circumcised Israel's heart (30:6).

(b) Paul connects the exceedingly uncertain 'blessing' promised to obedience to the law with the 'blessing' promised to Abraham by an unconditional word of God (Gal. 3:8ff.). The fact that the law was given so much later than the Abrahamic promise is taken to indicate the law's subordinate position (3:17–18). And, with a triumphant flourish, Paul points out that the promise to Abraham was not just of blessing for Israel, but for 'all the nations' (3:8), in consequence of which he makes the claim that this promise was a prophetic preaching of the Gospel (i.e. of his Antiochene Gospel): only now, with the glad welcoming of the Gentiles on equal terms, is the promise fulfilled (3:14).

(c) The Law itself had a demonstrably temporary nature, Paul believes. It was like a tourniquet applied in the ambulance to stop the bleeding until the patient could be properly sewn up (3:15). It was revealed through a prophetic intermediary (Moses) who received it from further mediators (angels – cf Deut. 33:1; Acts 7:38), but God's purpose is that his people should be immediately united to himself (Gal. 3:19b–20): 'through the law I died to the law *that I might live to God*' – the intermediaries have been removed at the law's own prompting. 'So that the law was our custodian until Christ came, that we might be justified by faith' (3:24).

(d) The very fact of the death of Christ shows that righteousness and life could not be attained through the Law (3:21–2). But paradoxically the Law actually promised life, as Paul admits in 3:12 by quoting Leviticus 18:5. His opponents naturally made much of this promise, which must have seemed to them to prove their case and disprove Paul's. In Galatians Paul contents himself with pointing out, as under (a) above, that the Law itself puts no confidence in its own promise. In Romans he goes into this in more detail – for the claim to give life itself does apparently make the law more than merely a temporary expedient supplied until life could be gained through Christ (Gal. 3:21f.). In Romans 7:7f. he argues that the 'holy and *dikaios* and good' law (7:12), which really 'promised life' (7:10 – a reference to Lev. 18:5), had been

taken captive by sin and made to serve precisely the opposite
end, death (Rom. 7:8–11). He uses the phrase 'the law of sin
and death' to pinpoint the reality of its bondage (8:2). But the
phrase is set in parallel to another, namely 'the law of the Spirit
of life in Christ Jesus', which '*has set me free from* the law of
sin and death'. It seems likely that this parallel phrase is
intended to describe the Law in a new bondage – to Christ and
the Spirit – in and through which it is able to fulfil its original
promise. This thought is confirmed when we turn to the
famous passage in Romans 10:4–5 NIV, where, after his
amazing statement 'Christ is the end of the law unto
dikaiosunē for everyone who believes' – which seems to
confirm his opponents' worst suspicions – Paul goes on to
quote their proof-text in his own support! 'For (unaccountably
omitted by RSV) Moses writes about the righteousness from
the law that "the man who does them shall live by them" (Lev.
18:5)'. C. E. B. Cranfield is surely right to suppose that Paul is
referring to Christ here.[7] Rightly understood, Leviticus 18:5
points ahead to Christ as the only one who has ever entered
into the life promised by the Law to the obedient, so that he is
the 'end' of the law in the same sense as he is the 'end' of the
promise to Abraham, by being 'the offspring . . . to whom the
promise had been made' (Gal. 3:19). Christ's resurrection,
therefore, is the proof that God has not rescinded his word
given in the Law. To seek to enjoy a *personal* fulfilment of that
promise, as Paul's opponents do, is to fail to recognise God's
righteousness in Christ (Rom. 10:3), indeed, to wish that
Christ had never died and been raised (Rom. 10:6–7). Paul's
opponents have no theology of the cross.

2   *The Death of Christ*

Paul's opponents saw the righteousness of God in his election
of Israel and gift of the Law, which then laid that righteousness
out for his people to imitate. Paul, on the other hand, saw it in
Christ and particularly in his death. Romans 3:21–6 is a vital
paragraph for our appreciation of the connection which he

saw between 'righteousness' and Christ's death. As a paragraph it plays much the same role within Romans as Galatians
2:16–21 – stating the whole thesis of the letter in a nutshell as
the 'text' for what follows.

The phrase 'the righteousness of God', which we have
already met in Romans 10:3 and which occurs three times in
this short paragraph, is much disputed by scholars. One
problem is to determine how and in what sense the phrase may
be applied to *man*, as is plainly the case in Romans 1:17 and
3:22. Another is to decide whether, applied to God, it refers to
a personal quality of his or to his saving activity (cf pp. 33–4),
or to his vindication as Saviour before the Church and the
world. Often modern analyses seek to distinguish between
things which Paul would have held together, and this is likely
to be the case here.

Paul's consideration of 'righteousness' in this passage begins
in 3:20 with a quotation of Psalm 143:2, which we have
already encountered in Galatians 2:16. For the purposes of his
struggle to attain a proper Christian understanding of the Law,
Paul feels compelled to emphasise that side of the tension in the
Psalms; the Psalmist who declared 'no man living is righteous
before thee' (143:2) possessed the law like any other Jew. But
he appealed to God not on the basis of his *gifts*, but of his
righteousness: 'In thy faithfulness answer me, in thy righteousness! Enter not into judgment with thy servant . . .' (143:1–2).
Paul proclaims the answer to this prayer in Romans 3:21ff.:
'But now the righteousness of God has been manifested apart
from the law, although the law and the prophets bear witness
to it . . .'. By simply resting upon God's saving righteousness,
and by associating himself beyond the borders of Israel with all
men, who are all alike unrighteous, the Psalmist 'bears witness'
to a righteousness of God 'apart from the law', however
strange or even blasphemous this might seem to Paul's opponents. And of course, when such a righteousness is forthcoming, it will thus apply beyond the borders of Israel to
all men, which is precisely what Paul maintains in Romans
3:28–30.

It seems, then, that on all four occasions where 'the righteousness of God' is used here (Rom. 3:21,22,25,26) it has the same basic significance – namely, God's saving righteousness, his intervention in a saving act on behalf of his people. Its application to men in verse 22 is possible because this righteousness is outgoing, catching men up into itself through faith, 'justifying' them freely by grace (v. 24). The passive form of the verb *dikaioō*, therefore, found in verses 20, 24 and 28, means 'to be an object of the saving righteousness of God (so as to be well-pleasing to him at the judgment)'. This saving righteousness God has 'demonstrated actively and effectively' (this is the force of the word *endeixis*, used twice in verses 25 and 26 and rather weakly translated 'show . . . prove' in RSV), by providing a wonderful 'remission of former sins' (v. 25b: RSV is almost certainly wrong with 'passing over'). The result of it all is that he has expressed his own righteousness by the salvation, the acquittal, of the one who believes in Jesus (v. 26).

But we have still skirted the heart of this passage. The reference to the 'remission of former sins' remains rather obscure until we note another way in which Paul is asserting here the testimony of the law to God's righteousness in Christ and its 'end' in him: God, through the death of his Son, has carried out in a final, climactic way the ritual of the Day of Atonement prescribed in Leviticus 16. Once a year the High Priest was commanded to enter the Holy of Holies and sprinkle sacrificial blood on the covering of the ark, known as the 'mercy-seat', in order to make full atonement for all the sins of Israel. Jews in Paul's day laid emphasis on the retrospective effect of the Day of Atonement, covering the sins of the past year.[8] But God has now provided a new 'mercy-seat' in the person of his Son (the word translated 'expiation' in RSV, *hilastērion*, is used by the Septuagint for 'mercy-seat' in Leviticus 16 and should probably be so translated here), a new place where a final and supreme atonement is made for all 'former sins', this time by the presentation of the blood of Christ himself. This is how God puts into effect his righteous purpose to save!

Paul thus made up for his opponents' lack of a theology of the cross by taking the cross as central in his own teaching. 'If righteousness were through the law, then Christ died to no purpose' (Gal. 2:21) marks the start of a train of thought which turns the cross from a puzzling embarrassment into a glorious vindication and fulfilment of God's purposes for Israel. The fact that the death of Christ can – indeed, *must* – be understood in terms of Israel's central act of worship prescribed by the Law means, first, that *the Law* is caught up and 'established' in Christ (Rom. 3:31) and secondly, that *Israel herself* is the primary object of 'the righteousness of God' in Christ. We can see the way in which Paul is moving in order to dispute his opponents' arguments 3 and 4 (p. 40) and vindicate the Antiochene practice.

3   Union with Christ

The principle expressed in Galatians 2:20 is basic to Paul's doctrine of justification: 'Christ who lives in me'. This way of putting it is quite unusual for Paul; he would normally say 'I live in Christ!' He perhaps puts it this way round here because of the representative nature of his testimony (see p. 44): Israel is to be brought to life by the life of the Messiah within her. But first she must die. If she insists on life on her own terms, she will die anyway; but if she 'dies to the law' willingly, she will live – yet not she: Christ within her. This point Paul expands in Galatians 3 in a remarkable way. He takes the central fact of Israel's election, on which she rested as the basis of her confidence before God, and *applies it instead to Christ*. His argument in 3:16 is fully in the Rabbinic style familiar to his opponents. The promise was given to Abraham 'and to his offspring'; because 'offspring' is a singular noun, we must understand it to refer to a single person, and the obvious candidate is Messiah. Israel must give up her claim to be herself the recipient of God's promises as Abraham's corporate 'offspring', and recognise that there is a prior claimant. But this is actually the way to inheritance of the position she has given up, for 'if you are Christ's then you are Abraham's offspring, heirs according to promise' (3:29). Incorporation into Christ leads to enjoyment of the inheritance which is rightly his.

For Paul's opponents the gift of the Messiah was the icing on the cake or the concluding paragraph of the book – that which simply added the finishing touch to God's purpose with Israel. For Paul there existed no cake or book apart from the Messiah. But once this was seen, the door was opened to include Gentiles as well as Jews in the offspring of Abraham. Scripture itself pointed ahead to this inclusion (3:8), which Paul triumphantly announces in 3:28: 'There is neither Jew nor Greek... for you are all one *in Christ Jesus*'. So Jews must find spiritual life 'like a Gentile' (2:14), abandoning trust in a special position conferred by 'works of the law' in order to become the objects of God's saving righteousness *through faith in Christ* (2:16). Only through such death comes life.

4   The Meaning of 'Faith'

A consideration of this vital theme will round off our study of Paul. Again the emphasis which is laid in Galatians 2:16, 20 is developed in chapter 3, where the coming of the Messiah is explained as the coming of 'faith' (vv. 15, 23, 25). The arrival of 'faith' introduces something radically new into the world, although it was foreshadowed in Abraham (vv. 6–9): up to that point 'the Scripture locked all things up under sin, in order that the promise, which is inherited only through the faith of Jesus Christ, might be given to those who have faith' (v. 22, paraphrased). The Law was a guard, keeping the people of God from harm 'until faith should be revealed... until Christ came' (vv. 23–4). But now they need the guard no longer, 'for you are all sons of God, through the faith which is to be found in Christ Jesus' (v. 26: preferable to RSV).

Paul gives a clue to his meaning at the beginning of Galatians 3: 'Did you receive the Spirit by works of the law, or by hearing with faith?' he asks the Galatians (v. 2), and then proceeds to work out this contrast between the period of the Law and that of faith, ushered in by the Messiah. It seems best to expound him as follows: in the person of the Messiah himself, and then in the company of all who are united with him and recipients of his Spirit (i.e. all who are 'justified'), there is to be found a new principle of life, a new 'faith' or 'faithfulness' (the Greek word *pistis* means both), a new obedience towards God (Rom. 1:5 and 16:26 both use the phrase 'the obedience of faith'; cf also Rom. 6:17), and a new love for him (cf Rom. 5:5), the *absence* of which had previously scuppered the Law as a system of salvation. Here we may develop the argument above about Romans 7:7ff. and 10:4–5 (pp. 45–6): the Law was released from its bondage to sin and found its 'end' in Christ, because he, who is the righteousness of God in person, gave to the Law the obedience which none other had given; and also because he now consequently forms the Messianic centre of a people in whom the same *pistis* is growing through union with him by his Spirit.

This is a rather unusual interpretation, but there is much to commend it. It fits Galatians 3 like a glove. Of course 'faith' also connotes a personal confession of Christ, as for instance in Romans 10:8–10, which probably reminds the Romans of their baptismal confession. But even here it is clear that faith means much more than merely a commitment to believe certain things about Christ: for Paul emphasises both that faith is a matter of *heart* and *lips*, which were the two focal points of the whole human personality according to ancient thought, and also (very dramatically) that the baptismal confession, the 'word of faith which we preach' (v. 8), is identical with the 'word' of the Law as described in summary by Moses in Deuteronomy 30:11–14. This stunning claim is plainly based upon the belief that the same righteousness of God that is expressed in person in Christ is also expressed in writing in the Law, so that the belief that God raised Jesus from the dead (i.e. gave him the life promised to complete obedience), and the confession of him as Lord, amount to an inner affirmation of the essence of the Law – which is precisely what Deuteronomy and the prophets complained was *not* forthcoming from Israel.

The same thought is expressed in Romans 8:3–4. The whole purpose of Christ's incarnation and sacrificial death was to 'condemn sin in the flesh' – that is to break the power of sin within our bodily, earthly existence – 'in order that the *dikaiōma* of the Law might be fulfilled in us, who walk not according to the flesh but according to the Spirit'. *Dikaiōma*, translated as 'just requirement' by RSV, does not mean the just demand of the Law that we should die for our sins, but summarises in one word the whole moral, decretal force of the Law, which is now to be fulfilled in those led by the Spirit of Christ. We see Paul giving Christian ethical application to this understanding of the Law in Galatians, where he first declares that neighbour-love is the fulfilment of the whole law (5:14) and then calls this law 'the law of Christ' as he urges his readers to 'bear one another's burdens' (6:2).

This is to argue that faith is an expression of righteousness; that it is the foretaste in our present experience of that full righteousness which will be realised at the end; that the expression 'justified by faith' (Rom. 5:1, etc) does not link two separate entities, righteousness and faith, making the latter the condition for the former, but describes one whole experience of membership of God's people. Paul thus finds it natural to apply 'righteousness' terminology to the present ethical 'walk' of the Christian: he emphasises in Romans 6 that baptism means that we have become 'slaves of righteousness' (v. 18) and must accordingly seek to live righteously (vv. 13, 19). The inner basis of this practical righteousness is to be 'obedient from the heart to the standard of teaching to which you were committed' (v. 17) – i.e. *faith*.

We may summarise our consideration of Paul by returning to Galatians 2:19–21. If we have interpreted him correctly, we should paraphrase these verses as follows:

I have been crucified with Messiah; but I live! Yet my life is not my own, but the life of Messiah within me. I live in two spheres simultaneously: I have an earthly, fleshly existence, which has now been caught up into the sphere of the faith to be found in and through the Son of God. This new life arises, as I say, from the death of Messiah, who loved me and gave himself up to death as the servant of the Lord on my behalf. I do not nullify the grace of God, as I have been accused! For if righteousness comes to God's people simply through their possession of his Law, then Messiah died to no purpose.

The death of the Messiah called Israel to radical self-criticism and reappraisal. Paul felt that his own apostleship to the Gentiles was the spearhead of that reappraisal. There can be no doubt that his theological grounding of that apostleship was a fantastically brilliant achievement, although there is no evidence to suggest that his opponents were convinced. Luke tells us that in Antioch believers were for the first time called 'Christians' (Acts 11:26). The appearance of this title must have delighted Paul (Did he invent it?) as much as it roused the suspicions of believers in Jerusalem. For them, it reflected a dangerous separatism; for him, it must have beautifully expressed Israel's death and resurrection into a new people of God gathered around the 'Christ', who summed up all the gifts of God to Israel in himself and then offered them freely to all men alike, Jews and Gentiles. 'Righteousness' was for both Paul and his opponents the key term in this argument about the proper definition of the people of God, for both believed that God's action to form a people for himself expressed his righteousness, and that this righteousness would then characterise the life of his people. But that was virtually the only common ground between them!

Conclusions about Righteousness

For ourselves, as we look back over the ground we have traversed, we can see how Paul gives a theological explanation for the tension which we found in Matthew and the Psalms. The basis of the whole life of the people of God is his righteousness – his outreaching, saving mercy which rescues his creation for himself. This righteousness has now been supremely expressed in Christ. But as men are grasped by it, 'justified' and made acceptable to God, so they are stamped with the image of their righteous Saviour, and summoned to

live in imitation of him as his people. 'Righteousness' thus
becomes a matter of human character and behaviour. This is
why it is perfectly natural for Matthew to place the caring
righteousness of God's people alongside the eternal saving
purpose of God as the two-poled ground for entry into eternal
life (25:34–5). Paul does exactly the same when he insists first
in Romans 2:13 that 'the doers of the law will be justified', and
then in 3:21 that 'the righteousness of God has been manifested apart from the law'; or when he argues in 5:1 that our
justification is a past certainty, but then prays in Philippians
1:9–11 that his readers may increase in love, knowledge and
discernment, 'so that you may approve what is excellent, and
may be pure and blameless for the day of Christ, filled with the
fruits of righteousness . . .'; or when in 3:8–12 the gift of
righteousness through faith in Christ does not relieve Paul of,
but calls him to, a struggle to attain to the resurrection of the
dead.

This is a very subtle aspect of biblical theology (the same
balance can be found in the Old Testament) which it would be
very easy to misstate or distort. Particularly for Protestant
Christians, the position described here looks uncomfortably
like synergism, the belief that we can contribute to our own
salvation. Nothing could be farther from the truth! We do not
add something lacking in the righteousness of God which has
made us his. The difficulty for us Protestants arises from the
distinction between 'justification' and 'sanctification' which
we have inherited from our fathers in the faith: the view that
justification is heavenly and decretal, changing our *status*
before God from 'sinners' to 'righteous', while sanctification is
earthly and gradual, changing our *state* in ourselves likewise
from 'sinners' to 'righteous'. In the former we are definitely
passive, in the latter active. In its insistence that salvation is all
of God, this scheme is unsurpassable. But there are three
weaknesses in it:

1   It does not correspond to Pauline vocabulary. Paul scarcely
uses the word 'sanctification', and does not distinguish it from
the 'righteousness' vocabulary when he does (see e.g. Rom.
6:19–22). In fact this traditional Protestant doctrine while

claiming to represent Pauline thought invests his vocabulary with un-Pauline emphases. Recently J. A. Ziesler has sought to vindicate Protestant teaching by claiming that Paul distinguishes between a doctrine of *justification* and a doctrine of *righteousness*, equivalent to the traditional distinction between justification and sanctification.[9] He argues that Paul uses the verb *dikaioō* in connection with the former, and the noun *dikaiosunē* and adjective *dikaios* for the latter. His work is excellent, particularly his discussion of the relationship between the themes of righteousness and union with Christ; but he does not supply anything to satisfy the enquiring mind which asks whether there was not an inner theological connection which enabled Paul to use words from one word-group in such apparently different senses; and his distinction does not fit well passages like Galatians 2:16–21 and Romans 3:20ff., where verb and noun/adjective are used in close connection.

2   It misses a whole area of biblical thought which is vital for Paul, namely the significance of 'the righteousness of God' as God's *saving* righteousness actively directed at the rescue of his Creation. Although this is plain to see in the Old Testament, its significance for Paul has only recently been explored and does not form part of the traditional Protestant doctrine.

3   Though it is easy to show how, in the life of a believer, sanctification is the natural consequence of justification, it has always been hard for Protestant theology to show the *theological* necessity for sanctification. The accusation has been made repeatedly – sometimes directed at Paul – that it is hard to deduce moral imperatives from a solely heavenly, declaratory justification. A man who has been declared righteous by God in his sovereign grace may well – nearly always does – feel obliged, out of deep thankfulness, to a life of obedience. But is the appropriateness of thankfulness the only *logical* basis for obedience in Pauline or biblical thought? The exposition of that thought proposed here provides a much more solid basis by trying to trace *one* doctrine of righteousness which embraces all uses of the term.

If the understanding of righteousness outlined here is correct, then not only have we discovered a unified framework in which the whole biblical doctrine of righteousness can be held together, but also discovered the basis upon which 'justification' descends from its theological ivory tower and becomes a vital, everyday matter for the life of each Christian. It is the conviction that that is its proper place which, above all else, unites the contributors to this volume.

3

JUSTIFICATION BY FAITH: A TRUTH FOR OUR TIMES

James Atkinson

(This chapter was first given in the form of two College lectures by the author at Oak Hill in December, 1980.)

A Summary of the Gospel

It is true that the phrase 'justification by faith' became a polemical party cry of the sixteenth century. It is equally true that it has often played that role among evangelicals these 400 years. But our sixteenth-century Reformers saw the phrase as a summary of the Gospel, expressing a New Testament doctrine that originated in the Old Testament and was preserved down the centuries by the great Church fathers. Cranmer, for example, makes this abundantly clear by the patristic authorities he cites in the *Homily on Salvation*.

The phrase summed up the Gospel: it was no innovation, it was a renovation. It was no party cry; it was the clarion call of scholarly evangelical churchmen, within a secularised, institutionalised, despiritualised Church, to grasp and then proclaim the Gospel of grace in Christ in authentic New Testament language.

The doctrine means that a man is saved by faith in Christ only, through the grace of God, and not by any works or human merit. The doctrine deals with the first and last question of man: how do I stand in relation to God? It speaks of the paradox of how God handles man, man who knows his estrangement from God, his alienation from the mystery of being. In those devastating words of Luther, *'wir handeln nicht, sondern wir werden gehandelt'* (it is not we who handle this matter, it is we who are handled by God). To express it in other words: it is not a question of asking ourselves what we are going to do about this distance from God which every man feels, but of opening ourselves to what God has done, and is doing, to create a new relationship in which he and we are together.

From the very beginning God has been seeking to establish a living relationship between himself and sinful man. This is the story of the Bible, of man's failure to respond to God, narrowing down through the centuries to one man, Jesus Christ. Christ is the author and perfector of our faith in that he showed in his own perfect faith and obedience what constitutes a proper human relationship to God. Unlike Christ, man as sinner cannot know that relationship. The moment a sinner sees that truth, however, and looks to Christ rather than trying to create communion with God by his own efforts, he is saved.

Luther's formula for this was *sola fide*. He is criticised in Calvinist quarters for putting the question in the wrong way, an egocentric way: *'Wie soll ich ein gnadigen Gott finden?'* (How shall I find a gracious God?). For Luther it was bound to be put that way, for he entered the monastery to save his soul. He thus set off, we may agree, on an egocentric mission, but like Saul, who went out to look for a couple of lost asses and returned with a kingdom, Luther gained not only his own soul, but the long-lost treasure of the New Testament and the Gospel. Calvin came a generation later, and rightly set justification in its true theocentric orbit. He traced the doctrine back to God's eternal election as the ultimate ground of salvation and our only hope in life and death. But both he and Luther mean the same thing, and both re-declare the common Gospel, promised in the Old Testament, fulfilled in and by Christ, proclaimed in the Acts and the Epistles, and maintained by instinct if not always by intellect in the Church. The heart of the matter is that evangelical theology affirms *Salva-*

tion in Christ Only against any and all Pelagianism or synergism, which in varying degrees would divide the saving work and the saving merit between God and man. Luther taught that this *solo Christo, sola fide* (by Christ only, by faith only) was the doctrine by which the Church would stand or fall. Be that as it may, let it be said here that this central biblical and patristic doctrine on which the Church is built belongs not to Protestantism but to the whole Church. It was for substance the confession of Peter and the first creed of Christendom. It is the taproot of spiritual life and the heart of the ecumenical heritage.

It is one of the ironies of history to reflect on how close the entire Church was to re-accepting this evangelical doctrine in the sixteenth century. At the Diet of Regensburg in 1541 it was actually agreed on, but the papal curia consistently rejected it, and formulated its own theology at Trent. Reginald Pole, though clearly arguing in his *Treatise on Justification* (1569) that a man is saved by love in addition to faith, nevertheless always strove to retain the *sola fide* within the Catholic corpus. Thus, he once offered the spiritual advice 'to *believe* that faith only saves, but to *act* as if works only save'. It is surely a remarkable fact that in our time Hans Küng (*Rechtfertigung* (Justification), 1957) cannot find any irreducible distinctions between the evangelical and Catholic doctrines sufficient to divide the Church, and argues that these distinctions are just the marks of two theological schools. He sees *definitions* such as justification by faith as *confirmations*, which are strictly speaking dispensable, and whose existence can only be justified to the extent that they clarify understanding. Küng even concurs with the Thirty-Nine Articles.

Salvation by Works and Salvation by Faith

There are two ways of salvation discussed in the Bible.

(a) There is salvation in Christ only by faith, which was promised in the Old Testament, which Christ himself made possible, and which he commissioned the apostles to proclaim after it had been effected. This is salvation as set forth in the Gospel.

(b) There is salvation by obedience to the Law, by which obedience a man is thought to make himself acceptable to God. This was the way of salvation according to the Judaism in which Christ and his disciples were brought up, and of which St Paul was at first the zealous defender against the Gospel.

Christ moved men beyond this doctrine of salvation by merit, as Paul was also to do after his conversion. Christ had come not to call the righteous but sinners to repentance. He did not come as a rabbi to teach the Law, but as Messiah, to show men who loved the Law that had they understood the Law they would have seen it as a preparation for the Gospel: for if they had understood the righteousness of the Law they would have seen the need for the righteousness of the Gospel. When Christ spoke to them of the relationship between God and man, it was in terms of a lost son (Luke 15) who was saved not by his righteousness (he had none) but by the mercy and goodness of the father. The son could never on his own have restored the relationship he had broken. Again, the labourers in the vineyard (Matt. 20) were rewarded not in proportion to their work but by the graciousness of their master. So, too, the Pharisee (Luke 18:9ff.) was not justified for all his virtue and goodness, solid though these were, whereas the publican was justified because he was aware of his sin and hopelessness, and, having no hope in himself, he just cried to a gracious God. No man can have any claim on God. The same message was proclaimed to all: Repent and believe the Gospel. Christ shows that he knows man is rebellious and estranged from God in sin, and to restore this human estrangement required a move from God. Christ's own coming was that move, and it is in that sense fundamentally that he fulfilled the Old Testament. If the Old Testament is viewed from the point of God's gracious activity the New Testament appears as its perfect fulfilment.

This point may be illustrated by comparing the ministry of Christ with that of John the Baptist. John, too, preached a call to repentance, but his message left men in a state of exalted paralysis. When his bewildered converts asked John what they were to do now that they had repented and been baptised, all that John could offer was ethical advice: even John, although Jesus' cousin and the greatest of all born of women, belonged to another world, a religious world of law, merit, ethics. 'He who has two coats, let him share with him who has none; and he who has food, let him do likewise' (Luke 3:11). To the tax collectors he said, 'Collect no more than is appointed you' (v. 13): to the soldiers, 'Rob no one by violence or by false accusation; and be content with your wages' (v. 14). Repentance was to be expressed in doing, rather than in seeing and tasting new life.

But with Christ it was different. He showed his hearers that it was not advice (the Law) that they needed, but the saving Gospel of God. He spoke of a repentance that brings folk into the kingdom of God, of a God who through all the centuries has been gracious and merciful, of a God who loves and seeks sinners, of a God who offers the ultimate, himself as man, to redeem them. 'No man ever spoke like this man!' (John 7:46). 'All . . . wondered at the gracious words which proceeded out of his mouth' (Luke 4:22). '. . . for he taught them as one who had authority, and not as their scribes' (Matt. 7:29).

He was the self-authenticating Word of God, searching out the hearts of men. He brought a message of *salvation*, different from any they had ever heard before. It was not a call to do more and to do it better, but a call to listen more and to hear better. 'Take heed what you hear' (Mark 4:24); see what God purposes; attend to Christ, God's personal saving Word who by his personal ministry cleanses and renews. John had declared: '. . . but he who is mightier than I is coming . . . he will baptise you with the Holy Spirit and with fire' (Luke 3:16). This Spirit-and-fire baptism was to signify not only our repentance but a vivifying and cleansing rebirth from above: it would thus mark the transition from the Law to the Gospel.

This distinction between the dispensations of John and Jesus was given its ultimate elucidation by the apostles, for while Christ preached the Gospel, the totality of the new life could only be appropriated after the Crucifixion, Resurrection and Ascension. That is why one finds the clearest Gospel not in the four Gospels but in the Epistles. In the Epistles, and at its finest in Romans, Paul has defined the content of faith in Christ clearly and unequivocally for all time. He has fixed it by the total sweep of his account of what God in Christ has done, does and will do for the salvation of mankind lost in Adam. There is an important reason to focus on Paul at this point, namely that both intellectually and morally Paul was as outstanding a person as Judaism could produce. It was one thing for Jesus to preach free grace and justification by faith to dispossessed Galileans, the accursed 'people of the land', but it was quite another thing to convince official, self-righteous, conservative Judaism that the time was fulfilled and the Law fulfilled in the Gospel. Christ fought this fight, and it cost him his life. Of the Gospel writers only John focuses on this, with his emphasis on Christ's messages in the Temple at the feasts, and the Johannine debates reveal to us the full significance and implications of the Galilean preaching about Jesus' own person and place in God's kingdom. In the same way, it took a Hebrew rabbi, a Hebrew of the Hebrews, as touching the Law perfect, to tell the world what it meant for a man to be justified, not by the works of the Law, but freely by the grace of God. This is what was meant by justification by faith in Christ only. See now how Paul understood this doctrine.

The phrase 'justification by faith' gives expression to what is essentially new and distinctive in Christianity, differentiating it not only from its historical origin, Judaism, but from all other religions of the world. Paul saw two radically distinct doctrines of salvation in conflict. One, salvation by the works of the Law was a way of discipline, effort, ethic and self-righteousness. The other was a way for a sinner who, knowing he could never make himself righteous enough to be acceptable to God, would joyfully accept with both hands the free mercy which God offered to him. This made salvation now no longer a matter of man and his works, but God and his Work; no longer a matter of man and his righteousness, but of God and his Righteousness. Righteousness in Paul means a right relationship with God, whether earned by effort or gained by gift; and the righteousness of God is Paul's theological shorthand for both the act of God giving this gift to sinners through faith, and the gift itself (see Rom. 3:21–6; Phil. 3:9). So it was not a case of God being far removed and of man making efforts to reach him. It was the other way round. It was man who was far removed from God, and God who had come all the way in Christ to meet sinners, freely offering them unconditional forgiveness and a new life; a life hid with Christ in God.

It is important to stress at this point the *objectivity* of this deliverance, regarding which St John could write of 'that which we have heard, which we have seen with our eyes, which we have looked upon and touched with our hands, concerning the word of life' (1 John 1:1). We are not here in a world of subjective fancy, but of objective fact. The cross was a heavy baulk of timber, real enough and rough enough to tear the bearers' shoulders with splinters. The tomb was real enough to convince visitors of its emptiness. Jesus was real enough to defeat all the tyrants – wrath, sin, law, and even death – hand to hand, and to rise triumphant. Now faith grasps a living Lord. The human situation is like that of a man trapped in a bog: unless somebody comes along to give power and leverage from a base firmer than his, he will go under. Faith is not a self-generated, self-propelled source of leverage, but a relationship, and its power is really the power of the one with whom it relates. Faith is 'a free surrender and a joyous wager on the unseen, untried and unknown goodness of God.'[1] 'If you believe, you possess', said Luther, 'if you do not believe, you do not possess' – in other words, God becomes effective in our life as we believe in him.

Faith, says Paul, is a gift of God (Eph. 2:8). It is not something we put into the bargain: nor is it something for which you can strive. It is not credulity, neither is it a feeling. It is not a mystical intuition, neither is it a psychologically comfortable state of mind. It is not in essence assent to propositions. It is not the case that a man has faith and is thereby enabled to believe the Gospel. Rather it is that when this Gospel is proclaimed, faith is created and given by God in confrontation. Faith comes as a new kind of self-understanding: not a mere change of opinion, nor yet an act of the unconscious, but a movement in man's personal existence, brought about through an encounter with God. This is what Paul meant when he described the Gospel as the power of God unto salvation (Rom. 1:16). It wins, compels, changes, arrests: it makes a man aware of a new dimension. Hearing the Gospel as the gracious word of one's Creator, and of Christ, confronting and addressing one, is as much an *event* in a person's life as being confirmed, or getting married, or having a baby. It *happens*.

That is the meaning of objectivity in this context. When the Gospel is declared and heard, it brings faith with it. The Gospel is primary: when it is preached it awakens faith in us. When one hears the Gospel, and is conquered by it, that is faith. Küng writes:

> In justification the sinner can give nothing which he does not receive by God's grace. He stands there with his hands entirely empty. Just as Abraham in Genesis 15:6 and Romans 4:3 and as the Israelites before Moses in Exodus 4:31: 'And the people believed; and when they heard that the Lord had visited the people of Israel and that he had seen their affliction, they bowed their heads and worshipped.'

This man is a man who knows that he has nothing to build for God, but he accepts God's word, like David. 'Would you build me a house to dwell in? . . . Moreover, the LORD declares to you that the LORD will make you a house' (2 Sam. 7:5,11). This man is a man who will not dash off on a charger, but whose power lies in quietness and trust (cf Isa. 30:15–16). He receives the kingdom of God like a little child (Mark 10:15) and says nothing beyond a Marian 'let it be to me according to your word' (Luke 1:38). He is a man who expects nothing from himself, but expects all from God, and is completely open to that which is his only refuge. This is the man who does not work but believes, and for him all self-reliance and self-confidence are now ended. 'Then what becomes of our boasting? It is excluded. On what principle? On the principle of works? No, but on the principle of faith. For we hold that a man is justified by faith [alone] apart from works of law'

(Rom. 3:27–8; cf Rom. 4:2, 5–6; 9:30–2; 10:4–6; 1 Cor. 4:7; 2 Cor. 12:9). 'Yet (we) know that a man is not justified by works of the law but through faith in Jesus Christ, even we have believed in Christ Jesus, in order to be justified by faith in Christ, and not by works of the law, because by works of the law shall no one be justified' (Gal. 2:16; 3:6; Phil. 3:9; etc.).[2]

The Text behind 'Justification by Faith': Habakkuk 2:4

When Paul wanted to make this doctrine unequivocally clear he expressed it thus: *Ho (de) dikaios ek pisteōs zēsetai* (Rom. 1:17; Gal. 3:11). 'He who is righteous [justified] by faith shall live' is probably the meaning Paul intends, though the rendering 'He who is righteous [justified] shall live by faith' remains grammatically possible. These words had played a remarkable role in Jewish history and were to play a still more remarkable role in Christian history.

(a) They first occur in Habakkuk 2:4. Confronted by the Chaldean invader, who was to devastate their land and take the people of God into captivity, the prophet went to his watchtower to hear what God would say to him. God reassured him that the proud conqueror would one day fall, but 'the righteous shall live by his faithfulness [i.e. trust expressed in fidelity]'.

(b) In the synagogue this text played the significant role of a summary of the Law. The Talmudic tradition says that on Sinai Moses received 613 commandments, King David summed them up in 11 (Ps. 15), Isaiah summed them up in 6 (Isa. 33:15f.), Micah in 3 (Mic. 6:6–8), Isaiah again in 2 (Isa. 56:1), and, finally, Habakkuk in 1, 'the just shall live by faith [in the sense, again, of fidelity]'. This meant that the synagogue read the text as a summing up of righteousness by the Law and its works. To keep the Law was to lay hold of life: by such faith would the faithful live.

(c) Now Paul takes up this prophetic and hallowed word, which had originally called for righteousness by faithfulness to the Law and its works, and claims that it was designated *by God* to mean the righteousness not of the Law but of faith in

Paul's own sense. How could a rabbi handle the Word of God with such liberty, indeed as it seemed perversity? Paul would have explained his procedure as follows. As all the rabbis taught, Scripture has many meanings, and not all of them are immediately disclosed in the original historical context. As the Word of God, its meaning is not exhausted by what God said and did to and with the original recipients; by extending the situational context of interpretation, God's further acts reveal further significance in the words of his Word than could be seen before. Knowing that God had done a new thing in Christ, ushering in the new kingdom and the new life of the last days, Paul understood that God would have a correspondingly new word to say out of Scripture to those 'upon whom the end of the ages has come' (1 Cor. 10:11). To express it differently, Paul knew that the events of Scripture, which happened forward in the sequence of an unfolding divine purpose, must now be interpreted backward from Christ, their Omega point, from whom their ultimate significance derives. As Luther was later to say to Erasmus, *'Tolle Christum e scripturis, quid amplius in illis invenies?'* ('Take Christ out of the Scriptures; what more will you find in them?') So Paul could write: 'the Scripture, foreseeing that God would justify the Gentiles by faith, preached the Gospel beforehand to Abraham, saying, "In you shall all the nations be blessed"' (Gal. 3:8).

So while God's promise to Habakkuk had its own immediate significance, it also had a fuller meaning yet to be disclosed. In due time, the veil over Scripture was removed by Christ, and Paul saw that what God purposed to say through Habakkuk was what he was now saying through the apostle himself. In citing Habakkuk evangelically Paul interprets him Christianly. Paul's interpretation combines the two ideas of the righteous man (*dikaios*) and faith (*pistis*) into one, 'he who is righteous (right with God) is justified by faith', and it is this man who 'shall live'. Habakkuk was certainly speaking of righteousness by faithfulness to the Law, a faithfulness which equally certainly shows faith in God as vindicator and rewarder; but here Paul is saying that the ultimate meaning of Habakkuk's statement is fulfilled in the righteousness that comes by faith in the Gospel of Christ, for which the Law itself teaches us to look (see Rom. 3:21–2; 10:4).

Of course, Paul's case was not based on one text: he taught that the entire Old Testament spoke of, prophesied, and was ultimately fulfilled in a righteousness that came by faith not works. He argued his case from the Law, the Prophets and the Writings. For example, Abraham believed God, and it was counted to him for righteousness (Rom. 4:3, citing Gen. 15:6). Abraham was the man who 'did not weaken in faith'; 'no distrust made him waver concerning the promise of God'; he was 'fully convinced that God was able to do what he had promised'. Genesis 15:6 was 'written not for his sake alone, but for ours also' – for righteousness shall be reckoned to us too if we believe (Rom. 4:19–24). It had been God's clear intent all along, so Paul argues, that man should be justified not by obedience to the Law, but by faith, trust, and confidence in God and his promises.

Finally, Paul anchored this truth of justification by faith in the further truth that salvation is by God's promise and election: 'it is not of him that willeth nor of him that runneth, but of God that sheweth mercy' (Rom. 9:16, AV). This he argued by showing that not all the seed of Abraham are the children of promise 'that God's purpose of election might continue, not because of works, but because of his call' (Rom. 9:11). Jacob was chosen, Esau was not: and they were twin brothers.

Some Misunderstandings

The doctrine of justification by faith has been clouded by certain misunderstandings which are worth clearing up.

(a) *James and Paul* This theology has in the past been commonly muffled or countered in the Church of Rome by appeal to James's argument (Jas. 2:14ff.) that faith without works is dead, and that Abraham was justified by his works. The answer is simple, however. In the first place, being justified means for Paul being accepted by God, while for James it means being proved genuine. Also, 'works' and 'faith' in James and in Paul mean entirely different things. To James in this passage (where he seems to be quoting the words of others) 'faith' means orthodoxy, professed assent to truth: to Paul, the total commitment of body and soul to Christ. James is saying that unless the faith one professes *issues* in the fruit of good works directed to one's neighbour, it is a dead thing, no true faith at all. That Paul also said, and Christ before him. But to Paul the word 'works' means the works of the Law in doing which a man claimed justification, acceptance by God. This was the collision point of Christ against Judaism, and of Paul against the Judaisers, even when these included Peter and James and the pillars of the Church. James is protesting against a formal orthodoxy, the mere holding of opinions which bear no fruit in Christian conduct. Paul is protesting against Judaisers who make the Law a precondition of the Gospel. Luther, though he misunderstood James, was always sensitive to this distinction: 'Faith alone justifies', he said, 'yet faith is never alone. It is never without love; if love is lacking, neither is there faith, but mere hypocrisy'.

A further point may be added here. What has given force to the appeal to James is that post-Tridentine Roman Catholicism has always demanded the performance of meritorious works and good deeds alongside the receiving of God's saving work in Christ. This doubtless modifies the simplicity of justification by faith in Christ only: Roman Catholic theologies have never felt easy with the Pauline doctrine. It is worth reminding ourselves, too, that the natural man does not take easily to the doctrine either, particularly if he is cultivated, educated and moral. The natural man has a tendency (with Rome) to believe that essentially it is his own decency, his own efforts, and his own doing that restore him to God, or at least go a long way towards it. This is why Catholic theology tends to emphasise the Church where the evangelical theology emphasises Christ. Paradoxically, to preach faith in Christ only gives a purer doctrine of the Church as well as unloosing the power of the Gospel. The Gospel always tends to dissolve the institutional Church, the institutionalism of which always in its turn tends to destroy the Gospel; perhaps the true Church will have to tolerate the empirical Church till the end of time.

(b) The final judgment in Matthew 25   Another passage not infrequently raised against the Pauline doctrine is the trio of parables of the Last Judgment in Matthew 25 (the bridesmaids, the talents, the sheep and goats) in which people are ultimately divided on a basis of works done. This does not argue that a man is justified by his works, for such a view is plainly contrary not only to the parable of the Labourers in the Vineyard (Matt. 20:1–16), but to all of Christ's teaching on forgiveness, mercy and grace. The chapter is simply saying what James emphasised later: the acid test of faith is the fruit of good works. A faith without works is empty talk. 'The tree is known by its fruit' (Matt. 12:33–7).

(c) Righteousness – imputed or imparted?   Here is a further historic point of difference between evangelical and Catholic theologians. Evangelicals teach that the plain and only meaning of the word 'justify' is to be accounted or deemed righteous, to have righteousness *imputed* to one, so that a relationship made abnormal by sin may be made normal again. Catholics teach that justification is not by 'faith alone' but by faith furnished with love, *fides caritate formata*. They teach that it is by the grace of God that a man is led to faith, by which they mean essentially assent to the beliefs of which the Roman Catholic Church is custodian and interpreter. It is taught that the one who assents to these beliefs is then ready for sanctifying grace, which, if lost, may be restored through the sacrament of penance. The necessity for justifying faith to be furnished with love is explained by the fact that when God forgives a sinner he cannot enter into fellowship with him in his sinful state. Hence, in justifying the sinner, God not only pardons him but makes him righteous in himself. Righteousness is not merely imputed, leaving the sinner sinful, but is *imparted*. God grants the sinner the love which is the fulfilling of the Law, whereby he becomes acceptable. In short, justification covers God's whole work of pardoning, sanctifying, and on this twofold basis finally accepting, the sinner, who thus is justified not by faith alone but by faith and love.

Luther's teaching seems closer to the New Testament, truer too to universal Christian experience. We sinners cannot now or ever attain any righteousness of our own: we merit and deserve only condemnation. But God in his mercy, while we are yet to his eyes and in our own self-awareness ungodly (Rom. 5:8), receives us to his side into fullest fellowship from the word 'go'. This is God's imputing of righteousness, his unqualified loving acceptance of us for Jesus' sake. Luther used to express it thus: *simul justus et peccator* (at one and the same time, right with God yet a sinner);[3] *semper peccator, semper penitens, semper justus* (always a sinner, always penitent, always right with God).[4]

The story of Luther's discovery of this precious truth is one of the loveliest of all time. He describes how he went into the monastery to save his soul, and how all the disciplines, the confessions, the absolutions never answered his need or spoke to his condition. The more aware he was of God and his purity, his righteousness, his transcendence, the more keenly he became aware of his own creatureliness, his own unrighteousness, his own mortal finitude. He knew he could never attain the righteousness God demanded, and that one day he would be bound to face God's destructive wrath. After long study and prayer he realised that it was not a matter of Martin's work but of God's work. God had so loved the world that he gave his only-begotten Son, that whosoever believes in him should not perish but have eternal life. Martin realised that the meaning of Christianity was not a matter of pilgrimages, fastings, good works, etc., but a simple capitulation in faith to God's work of salvation. 'When I saw that Law meant one thing and Gospel another', he said, 'I broke through'.

(d) Faith is not a meritorious work Faith is only ever understood as it is described theologically, in relation to its object. Descriptions of it as a mental act, or even a Christian virtue, are man-centred rather than relational, and regularly give the wrong idea. Faith is not a work that merits, but a realising of demerit, a negating therefore of all hope of merit, and an amazed awareness of divine mercy. Faith to Luther meant utter despair of everything, save Christ. When a man

realises that in the matter of his own salvation he has nothing and can do nothing, and in his self-despair looks Christward, he is then received by God, accepted and justified, simply and solely on the grounds that he accepts what is proffered. 'Faith' here means not an optimistic disposition nor a blind confidence about the future, but a specific realised relationship. 'Christian faith', the faith that Christians exercise, is precisely 'faith in Christ', hearing, seeing, trusting, taking, embracing, knowing, rejoicing. We are justified *per fidem propter Christum*, through faith as the means on account of Christ the meritorious source, whence our acceptance flows as we look to him and grasp hold of his word of promise. 'Faith is only the instrument by which righteousness is received and cannot be confounded with Christ, who is the material cause, and at once author and dispenser of so great a benefit' (Calvin).[5] Active, responsive righteousness on our part then follows, as we have seen, wrought in us by Christ through his Spirit; but just as faith must not be confused with Christ, so neither must the righteousness that is imputed – i.e. acceptance – be confused with the righteousness that is thereafter imparted – i.e. good works – even though it is through Christ (in two different ways, however!) that both come. The former is ours through Christ's atoning death, the latter through his risen life; and the latter, for which sanctification is the accepted name, is the work of the Holy Spirit raising a man already justified by faith, not a contributing factor to man's justification. Sanctification like justification is by grace alone through faith alone.

Conclusion

From this exposition we can see now that the doctrine of justification by faith in Christ only is in truth the basis of Christianity. It is the key to the kingdom of heaven; it is the Gospel of peace and joy. A man who appropriates this truth is a man who has passed from danger to safety, indeed from death to life. A story is told of a traveller in Switzerland arriving on horseback in the middle of the night at an inn on the shores of Lake Constance, having lost his way during a great snowstorm. When the astonished innkeeper told him that the roads had all been impassable for days, and that he had actually ridden not along the road but over the frozen lake, the man blanched and collapsed in horror at the thought of how near to death he had been as his horse's hoofs had pounded, not the road, but the thin layer of ice on the lake's surface. The awareness of his justification by faith produces a similar reaction in the Christian man. He realises how very near he was to being lost in his former blind passage across the ice of his own efforts and works; in the warmth and light and safety of his place of refuge in Christ he contemplates how nearly lost he was, in spite of – indeed, in one sense because of – his brave and determined effort to travel. He takes fresh heart and goes on a saved man; a chastened man, but a believing man, a justified and joyful man. This is what real Christianity means.

Corollaries

Let us now explore some of the implications of this radical doctrine for the Church's ecumenical quest, its pastoral task, and the lives of its members.

1 Justification and the Bible

It is a significant fact how difficult scholars have found it to express in words Luther's main concern, to which the formula 'justification by faith alone' is pointing. When Lutheran scholars met at Helsinki in 1963 this was noticeable, as it also is in much of today's literature on Luther. Why should this be? The reason is that what justification by faith refers to is not a theoretical concept, like for instance Newton's laws, but the experience Luther knew of God active in grace. God met Luther as he studied Romans, and there he experienced what redemption is. From that experience he understood the whole Bible anew.

What is the Bible? It is in the first instance a set of testimonies to revelation in history. What is revelation? Revelation is the life and activity of God turned towards men, as he makes himself known to them in specific ways within specific relationships. God revealed himself to Moses, to the prophets, to the apostles, and their writings attest that revelation. And through their written word he reveals himself to us today as the same Lord. The Bible is the Word of God not merely by virtue of its inspiration (that is, its divine source), but also and indeed primarily because God by his Spirit still speaks its substance to his people, and always will. But the substance of the biblical witness is God actively redeeming through the cross of Christ and the promises based on it; both these realities being brought home with transforming power and, in the New Testament at least, clarity of understanding, to the witnesses who wrote the books. In other words, the justification of sinners by faith through Christ, as God's great saving work, is what the Bible is centrally about. This was what Luther came to see. We understand Luther only as we experience revelation in the way that he did, as the dynamic reality of God bringing home the word of justification to our hearts. And conversely, the question whether we have experienced revelation can be answered yes or no according to whether we are able to understand Luther!

Is justification by faith, then, the key to the Bible? Not in the sense of being a critical canon for judging its meaning and truth; but it does give interpreters perspective, for it shows us that the God of the Bible is the God whose constant and proper work is justifying sinners by grace through faith, whatever particular activities on his part any particular passages may celebrate. With that, it reminds us what the Bible really is – both as a whole and in its parts – namely, God's word of gracious self-disclosure, the word which God speaks to each reader and hearer every moment, and therefore at this very moment, to bring home to us his restoring mercy in Christ.

But Scripture is its own interpreter (*sui ipsius interpres*, as

Luther put it), and rather than speak of justification as its key it is better to say that one passage is the key to another, while the truth of justification by faith acts as a constant indicator of who and what God is, and of the centrality of Christ and of mercy in the divine self-revelation.

2   Christology and Certainty

Justification, we have seen, is central; and justification is in Christ. Justification by faith shows us, therefore, the significance of the Incarnation, which is twofold. Christ was both God come to save man and man living to God as he should, in filial obedience. He was man hearing, trusting and following God's word, demonstrating what it means to live by 'every word that proceeds from the mouth of God' (Matt. 4:4). He was, we may say, the great believer, the supreme man of faith; we might even say (though in one sense misleadingly, since he was no sinner) that he was truly and vicariously justified by faith. Certainly, had it not been for his perfect obedience of faith we could not be justified in him today. And as those who are justified in him, we may also properly say that our faith relies on his faith, both as that whereby his righteousness into which we enter was perfected (righteousness here meaning, as before, a right relationship with God) and as that which in our union with him undergirds and upholds our faith in the sight of God.

Egocentric doctrines of salvation focus on my faith, my decision, as if it were something of special value on which everything hinges, which therefore must be of adequate and acceptable quality. Thence springs the nagging doubt, is my faith good enough and strong enough to save me? Peace of mind is thus made impossible. But the Christocentric Gospel of the New Testament delivers us from the anxiety and uncertainty that these egocentric distortions create. True faith knows itself empty and weak, like the Oxfam child standing with an empty can. Our prayer, if real and honest, will never get beyond 'Lord, I believe – help my unbelief!' Yet our faith in its conscious weakness can be confident, for Christ's life of perfect faith guarantees to us God's faithfulness in mercy, and in Christ we are delivered from the power of darkness and translated by divine power into the care-less life of the kingdom of God's dear Son (Col. 1:13).

Christ by faith, as our appointed kinsman-redeemer taking responsibility for us, wrought righteousness on our behalf in both his living and his dying, and thus secured our absolute and abiding acceptance with the Father, whatever ambiguities and fears and diffidences and doubts may attach to our own faith. To proclaim this is the glory of true incarnational theology.

So we look for life exclusively to Christ. That is the reference of the Reformers' expressions – slogans, as they became – *sola fide, sola gratia, sola scriptura, solo Christo*. We look away from ourselves altogether, in order to live out of Christ alone. We surrender not only our real badness, which can be hard, but with it our fancied goodness, which can be harder. According to Paul and Luther, what alienates us from God most of all is not the evil in us, but the pride (*hubris*, as the Greeks called it) which resolves to conquer it, and so work a passage to God. With self-confidence, grave or jaunty (but in either case showing unbelief of the word of God) this pride declines the pain of surrendering our goodness – pain which, be it said, far exceeds that of moral toil and ascetic self-torture. But readiness to surrender goodness is the heart of the courage of faith; and in that surrender, in which the ambiguity of good and evil in our life is conquered by an unambiguous acknowledgment that we cannot save ourselves, the unambiguous reality of eternal life becomes ours through the work of God in Christ.

In the same way, we set aside our goodness as believers, declining to see our justification as the beginning of a new self-righteousness. Whatever else sanctification is, it is not that. Neither this nor any other form of self-salvation will stand the scrutiny of Scripture for a moment. Sixteenth-century Protestants saw the dangers of synergist and co-redemptionist theology, and opposed the Romanists on the point, but these ideas still appear. The New Testament writers, however, and Luther and Calvin following them, find the exact antithesis to them in the doctrine of election, which rests salvation on the prior decision of God in Christ. 'You did not choose me, but I chose you' (John 15:16). The doctrine of election guards the Gospel against the corruptions of legalism ('I move God to accept me by what I do') and preserves a sound doctrine of the Incarnation (the Word became flesh in order to become the mediator, saving sinners), and thus it maintains the biblical integrity of evangelical faith.

It is in this manner that the message of justification, apostolically unfolded in terms of New Testament Christology, imparts stability and certainty both to our thinking and to our living and hence to our entire view of all that happens as we walk life's bumpy and bewildering road.

3   Natural Knowledge under Judgment

God's justifying work of grace calls into question not only all natural goodness but also all natural knowledge. It diagnoses both as work of the flesh. It applies this same diagnosis equally to natural scepticism, dogmatic ignorance, willed agnosticism and radical doubt, in which intellectual pride and self-sufficiency have come up with the conclusion that God is unknowable and life meaningless. 'If any man would come after me,' says Jesus, '*let him deny himself* and take up his cross and follow me' (Mark 8:34). This challenges the natural man to look away from all that he knows, or thinks he knows, as well as from all that he is, or thinks he is, and to allow Christ to introduce himself as the way, the truth, and the life, through whom we come to the Father (John 14:6). One must learn from Christ to be sceptical about one's scepticism, agnostic about one's agnosticism, and doubtful about one's doubts. And Christians must learn from Christ that their own theological statements must be tested by Christ. Our theological statements at best echo and explicate biblical witness, and they become ventures in natural self-assertion the moment we refuse to submit them to the Christ of biblical witness, in order to be tested by the reality of God's justifying grace as Christ sets it forth.

T. F. Torrance suggests that we should think of justification as *verification*, in other words, as standing in a critical relation to all that we say in order to show how much of it is true. This is to claim that the ultimate verification of whatever we regard as knowledge (using that word in the sense of ultimate truth about anything) is to be sought and derived from no other source than Christ himself, the Christ of the Gospel, the Christ who is known in God's act of justifying sinners.[6] The doctrine of justification by faith thus has startling relevance to modern theological and philosophical debate. It undercuts all that would relativise the Gospel; it does this by carrying the war into the enemy camp and relativising natural and secular knowledge first. It discloses that the natural mind is as dark as the natural will is bad in relation to God, and that we must deny our natural self-confidence in the realm of both thoughts and works. In both spheres we must be willing for Christ to give us what we need – wisdom in the one case and righteousness in the other, both being rooted in what he is as the mediator who brings alienated sinners to repentance and to God. Thus, by exalting Christ as the final criterion and ultimate source of all true wisdom and knowledge (Col. 2:3), the Gospel of justification challenges the world and revolutionises the Christian intellectually no less than morally.

4 Justification and Ethical Decisions

Christ reigns in and over the justified sinner, where self reigned before, and so his life now expresses a new impetus: his faith is active in love. This gives a distinctive character to his decision-making. Each decision, ideally, will stem from faith rightly apprehended and facts rightly measured, and be the product of an absolute loyalty related to a pragmatic choice. To a Christian the absolute is total loyalty to God in Christ rather than to any abstract principle, and the pragmatism is informed by the truth as it is known in Jesus. Faith does not alter facts, but it alters the dimension in which facts are estimated and weighed, and the depth at which they are comprehended. 'Sleep neither over your Bible nor your newspapers,' said Barth. 'And it is my prayer that your *love* may abound more and more, with *knowledge* and all *discernment*, so that you may *approve* what is excellent,' wrote Paul (Phil. 1:9–10).

This means that every ethical decision must be approached *de novo*. Living mechanically, by rules, is not living Christianly. Justified believers are delivered from legalism, but are not thereby surrendered to the fashionable secular conscience or lack of it, nor to individualistic licence. In the living Church (and justification is a call to community in the Church with the rest of the justified) we shall find rich resources of wisdom and precedent – Christian case law, you might say – to guide us. But since our grasp of the faith is always somewhat unsure and our mastery of the facts always partial and limited, since also we can neither assess our motives with confidence nor calculate consequences with certainty, we are cast back every time on the mercy and forgiveness of God – which is precisely what justification by faith means for ethical life. As our persons need to be justified by grace, so do the decisions and acts whereby we seek to show love to God and men. This was the point of the famous words in which Luther encouraged Melanchthon: 'Be a sinner, and sin bravely, but believe in Christ and rejoice in him even more bravely' (*esto peccator et pecca fortiter, sed fortius fide et gaude in Christo*).[7] Try his best, the believer sins still, and knows it; but he continues justified by faith despite all.

5   The Problem of Tradition and Traditions

As we know, one major Reformation debate concerned the authority of Scripture vis-à-vis that of tradition. Catholic polemicists – Eck, Cochlaeus, Emser, More – claimed that the Church has authority over Scripture, to expound, explain and even develop it. Luther, by contrast, argued for the supremacy of the Word over tradition, as judge of all our traditions.

(Not all know that at Trent such Catholic scholars as Pietro Bertano, Bishop of Fano, and Angelo Bonucci, General of the Servites, were with Luther here, and argued that 'all is contained in Scripture', and understood Trent's formula about tradition as a source of beliefs as referring to an exposition of Scripture, not an addition to it.[8])

The faith through which believers are justified is correlative to the Word of God. So the doctrine of justification frees men from the shackles of lesser authorities to test all preconceptions and all traditional ideas by the Word directly. The Reformation stands for the supremacy of Scripture over all tradition, and for theological activity as the repentant rethinking of traditions by the light of the biblically mediated revelation of God in Jesus Christ.

This principle applies however to more than debates with Rome about infallibility, transubstantiation, merit, the immaculate conception and the assumption of Mary; it applies to ourselves as Anglicans, even against ourselves. For instance, what of the recent tradition called synodical government? Does it not stifle all forms of the spiritual leadership for which the world and the Church long? What of the fact that whereas the weekday activities of Luther's parish consisted solely of Bible study and exposition, the average Church of England parish today invests its energies in Cubs, Brownies, Scouts and Guides, youth clubs and tennis, badminton, football, whist drives, sales of work, choirs and dramatic societies? How does the Word of God judge these traditions? Surely an understanding of justification by faith in Christ, and the concentration on the Word of God which this would bring, would change both the administration and activities of the Church of England drastically.

6 Pastoral Ministry and Christian Life

Justification by Christ is grounded on his sovereign substitution for us, obeying the Father and enduring judgment in our place; and on his substitutionary work all our worship, ministry and life as Christians rest. His humanity displaces ours in the Father's sight. The Church is his body, our ministry is his ministry taking the form of ours, our worship is his worship of the Father articulated in us, and our life is his life lived through us. Luther stressed the pure humanity of Jesus, as the divine Son who became man to be our priest, to take our side, atone for us, speak to God for us, and thus be 'our only Mediator and Advocate' for time and eternity. His emphasis knocked the bottom out of medieval sacerdotalism in his own day, and does so still. In the Church Christ is all, and must be so acknowledged.

It is fashionable to turn this point against Catholic sacerdotalism. But there is a Protestant sacerdotalism, a sacerdotalism we could say of the Word rather than of the sacraments, which is no less blameworthy. How long must congregations endure clergy whose preaching is an airing of their own views on society's problems – women's liberation, homosexuality, marriage, divorce, the Third World, the race problem, the prisons, the police? Is this Christ's ministry? Is this Christ speaking his Word through his human spokesmen? Is this the word of God, by which alone man lives? When the clergy's prayers are so full of their own personalities and idiosyncrasies that they are sermons rather than prayers, is this praying in and through Jesus Christ our Lord? In all worship and ministry the lordship, leadership and mediation of Christ must be acknowledged and expressed according to the Word, or it is not Christian worship, the worship of the justified, at all.

What, now, of the Christian life, which pastoral ministry seeks to foster? Reference was earlier made to the care-less, care-free existence of a man justified by faith, who in the power of the Spirit realises that it is the Father's good pleasure to give him the kingdom. Such a man is never anxious about his sin, nor is he concerned to measure his spiritual temperature by the thermometers of holy emotions or ecstatic experiences. He is simply a 'man in Christ'. '. . . forgetting what lies behind and straining forward to what lies ahead, I press on toward the goal for the prize of the upward call of God in Christ Jesus' (Phil. 3:13–14). This is his language. He understands what

Paul meant by 'present your bodies as a living sacrifice, holy and acceptable to God, which is your spiritual worship. Do not be conformed to this world, but be transformed by the renewal of your mind, that you may prove what is the will of God, what is good and acceptable and perfect' (Rom. 12:1–2). He experiences what Paul had in mind when he told the Corinthian Christians, 'since, in the wisdom of God, the world did not know God through wisdom, it pleased God through the folly of what we preach to save those who believe. For . . . we preach Christ crucified' (1 Cor. 1:21–3).

God has loved us and does love us, for Jesus said in his great prayer, 'You have loved them, as You have loved Me' (John 17:23). It follows that nothing, and no person, can alienate the Christian from his God (see Rom. 8:38–9). That relationship does not depend on a conversion experience, or any other experience: it cannot even be destroyed (though it may be impaired) by sin in his life. The Christian is God's; he (or she) belongs to him. The basis of this assurance lies not in ourselves, not in anything that we are, have, believe, or do, but simply in what God did for us in Christ. Now we bask in the knowledge of God's love and care. '. . . the hairs of your head are all numbered' (Matt. 10:30). 'Are not *two* sparrows sold for a penny? And not *one* of them will fall to the ground without your Father's will. Fear not, therefore: you are of more value than *many* sparrows' (Matt. 10:29, 31).

In justification a man knows he is accepted by God as he is; what ground then has he ever to reject himself or to feel unacceptable? In this assurance, a man in Christ quietly moves forward towards the goal of likeness to Christ and ultimate fellowship with him in eternity. He is not anxious; he trusts God's call. He will keep clear of legalism and avoid the tyranny of moral rules: he stands fast in the liberty with which Christ has set him free. But his faith will issue in spontaneous love, the love of adoring gratitude to his God and Saviour. By this true faith is known. Jesus said: 'If you love me, you will keep my commandments' (John 14:15). The justified person will want to show his love for Jesus by doing just this.

7   The Prayer of the Justified

The doctrine of justification has implications also for prayer. There is no need for the Christian to bombard God: that is the mark of the pagan (Matt. 6:7). Prayer for the justified is talking to God in Christ's name, and such prayer is heard before the request is made.

When Satan tempts, trying one way or another to block our access to God and make us despair of ever regaining it, the Christian can confront him as Christ did in the wilderness, for he is a liar, a deceiver and, ultimately, a murderer. Satan cannot win, in fact he has already been defeated. So there is no need to fear him. Nor, for that matter, is there any reason to fear death itself, for as Paul tells the Romans, 'being justified by faith, we have peace with God through our Lord Jesus Christ: by whom also we have access by faith into this grace wherein we stand, and rejoice in hope of the glory of God' (Rom. 5:1–2 AV).

Few men have been better qualified to speak about prayer than Luther. Knowing that he was justified by faith, he prayed continuously and incessantly, knowing that God would hear his every thought, his every prayer, his every intercession. He prattled to God all day long, like a child on a walk with its parent. He prayed with a certainty and confidence that God would hear him and help him, knowing that his prayer in the name of Christ was acceptable to the Father. He remains a model for us all.

8   The Challenge to the Church

Now the threads must be drawn together.

Society is sick. Secularised, permissive, pluralist, resolutely and ruthlessly oriented to achievement and success, and disillusioned about its own materialism, it is far from being the different and better world that we came out of the Second World War resolved to build. Was there ever, then, a more opportune moment for proclaiming God's mercy in Christ?

No truth would be heard more gladly today than the good news of God who justifies sinners by faith only. No truth would be more beneficial to society were its implications spelled out in, for instance, the fields of counselling and human relations. To an uncertain, apprehensive world where so many feel alienated, lost, lonely, unrelated, and fearful, surely this teaching about the new relationship which God creates, in which he may be totally trusted through good and evil alike because his love is known, and in which even evil is transmuted into the raw material of the good life, would come as music from heaven. Nothing would so warm the hearts of the lost and lonely, nothing would so steel the nerve of the fearful and hopeless, than to know that Christ prays for them as he prayed for faltering Peter: 'Simon, Simon, behold, Satan demanded to have you, that he might sift you like wheat, but I have prayed for you *that your faith may not fail*!' (Luke 22:31f.). To be sure, the Word would not come home without the Spirit making entrance for it into the darkened heart; but the Spirit is pledged to do precisely this when the Word is faithfully communicated, and in any case fear that the Word will be unfruitful is never a good excuse for not spreading it.

Is not the message of justification by faith only through Christ needed today? If so, the Church's task is plain: first to re-learn it ourselves (who can doubt that much needs to be done here?), and then to proclaim it, with prayer and hope, in the power of the Spirit. And when Jesus Christ has been given and is occupying his rightful place in the centre, as head and Lord of the Church, its only prophet, priest and king – which means, when our preaching, our ministry, our worship, and our congregational life shows that for us Christ is all, and that it is by his justifying mercy, known, trusted and adored, that we live – then the process will have begun. May we be given to see it in the midst of these decadent and desperate years.

4

JUSTIFICATION IN PROTESTANT THEOLOGY

Jim Packer

(We are grateful to the Presbyterian and Reformed Publishing Company of Philadelphia for permission to reprint some of this material which first appeared under their imprint.)

The Heart of the Gospel

'The confession of divine justification touches man's life at its heart, at the point of its relationship to God. It defines the preaching of the Church, the existence and progress of the life of faith, the root of human security and man's perspective for the future.'[1] So wrote G. C. Berkouwer of the doctrine of justification by faith set forth by Paul and re-apprehended with decisive clarity at the Reformation; and in so writing he showed himself a true heir of the Reformers. For his statement is no more, just as it is no less, than a straightforward spelling out of what Luther had meant when he called justification by faith *articulus stantis aut cadentis ecclesiae* – the point of belief which determines (not politically or financially, but theologically and spiritually) whether the Church stands or falls.

With Luther, the Reformers saw all Scripture as being, in the last analysis, either Law or Gospel – meaning by 'Law' all that exposes our ruin through sin and by 'Gospel' everything that displays our restoration by grace through faith – and the heart

of the biblical Gospel was to them God's free gift of righteousness and justification. Here was the sum and substance of that
*sola fide – sola gratia – solo Christo – sola scriptura–soli Deo
gloria* which was the sustained theme of their proclamation,
polemics, praises and prayers. And to their minds (note well!)
proclamation, polemics, praise, and prayer belonged together,
just as did the five Latin slogans linked above as epitomising
their message. Justification by faith, by grace, by Christ,
through Scripture, to the glory of God was to them a single
topic, just as a fugue with several voices is a single piece. This
justification was to them not a theological speculation but a
religious reality, apprehended through prayer by revelation
from God via the Bible. It was a gift given as part of God's total
work of love in saving us, a work which leads us to know God
and ourselves as both really are – something which the unbelieving world does not know. And to declare and defend God's
justification publicly as the only way of life for any man was at
once an act of confessing their faith, of glorifying their God by
proclaiming his wonderful work, and of urging others to
approach him in penitent and hopeful trust just as they did
themselves.

So, where Rome had taught a piecemeal salvation, to be
gained by stages through working a sacramental treadmill, the
Reformers now proclaimed a unitary salvation, to be received
in its entirety here and now by self-abandoning faith in God's
promise, and in the God and the Christ of that promise, as set
forth in the pages of the Bible. Thus the rediscovery of the
Gospel brought a rediscovery of evangelism, the task of sum-
moning non-believers to faith. Rome had said, God's grace is
great, for through Christ's cross and his Church salvation is
possible for all who will work and suffer for it; so come to
church, and toil! But the Reformers said, God's grace is
greater, for through Christ's cross and his Spirit salvation, full
and free, with its unlimited guarantee of eternal joy, is given
once and for ever to all who believe; so come to Christ, and
trust and take!

It was this conflict with the medieval message that occa-
sioned the fivefold 'only' in the slogans quoted above. Salva-

tion, said the Reformers, is by faith (man's total trust) *only*, without our being obliged to work for it; it is by grace (God's free favour) *only*, without our having to earn or deserve it first; it is by Christ the God-man *only*, without there being need or room for any other mediatorial agent, whether priest, saint, or virgin; it is by Scripture *only*, without regard to such unbiblical and unfounded extras as the doctrines of purgatory and of pilgrimages, the relic-cult and papal indulgences as devices for shortening one's stay there; and praise for salvation is due to God *only*, without any credit for his acceptance of us being taken to ourselves.

The Reformers made these points against unreformed Rome, but they were well aware that in making them they were fighting over again Paul's battle in Romans and Galatians against works, and in Colossians against unauthentic traditions, and the battle fought in Hebrews against trust in any priesthood or mediation other than that of Christ. And (note again!) they were equally well aware that the Gospel of the five 'onlies' would always be contrary to natural human thinking, upsetting to natural human pride, and an object of hostility to Satan, so that destructive interpretations of justification by faith in terms of justification by works (as by the Judaisers of Paul's day, and the Pelagians of Augustine's, and the Church of Rome both before and after the Reformation, and the Arminians within the Reformed fold, and Bishop Bull among later Anglicans) were only to be expected. So Luther anticipated that after his death the truth of justification would come under fresh attack and theology would develop in a way tending to submerge it once more in error and incomprehension; and throughout the century following Luther's death Reformed theologians, with Socinian and other rationalists in their eye, were constantly stressing how radically opposed to each other are the 'Gospel mystery' of justification and the religion of the natural man.

For justification by works is, in truth, the natural religion of mankind, and has been since the Fall, so that, as Robert Traill, the Scottish Puritan, wrote in 1692, 'all the ignorant people that know nothing of either law or gospel', 'all proud secure sinners', 'all formalists', and 'all the zealous devout people in a natural religion', line up together as 'utter enemies to the Gospel'. That trio of theological relatives – Pelagianism, Arminianism, and Romanism – appear to Trail as bastard offspring of natural religion fertilised by the Gospel. So he continued: 'The principles of Arminianism are the natural dictates of a carnal mind, which is enmity both to the law of God, and to the Gospel of Christ; and, next to the dead sea of Popery (into which also this stream runs), have, since Pelagius to this day, been the greatest plague of the Church of Christ, and it is like will be till his second coming.'[2] – a point of view entirely in line with that of Luther and his reforming contemporaries a century and half before. And all study of non-Christian faiths since the time of Luther and Traill has confirmed their biblically based conviction that salvation by self-effort is a principle that the fallen human mind takes for granted.

It has been common since Melanchthon to speak of justification by faith as the *material* principle of the Reformation, corresponding to biblical authority as its *formal* principle. That is right. Of all the Reformers' many biblical elucidations, the rediscovery of justification as a present reality, and of the nature of the faith which secures it, were undoubtedly the most formative and fundamental. For the doctrine of justification by faith is like Atlas. It bears a whole world on its shoulders, the entire evangelical knowledge of God the Saviour. The doctrines of election, of effectual calling, regeneration, and repentance, of adoption, of prayer, of the Church, the ministry, and the sacraments, are all to be interpreted and understood in the light of justification by faith, for this is how the Bible views them. Thus, we are taught that God elected men from eternity in order that in due time they might be justified through faith in Christ (Rom. 8:29f.). He renews their hearts under the Word, and draws them to Christ by effectual calling, in order that he might justify them upon their believing. Their adoption as God's sons follows upon their justification; it is, indeed, no more than the positive outworking of God's justifying sentence. Their practice of prayer, of daily repentance, and of good works springs from their knowledge of justifying grace (cf

Luke 18:9–14; Eph. 2:8–10). The Church is to be thought of as the congregation of the faithful, the fellowship of justified sinners, and the preaching of the Word and ministration of the sacraments are to be understood as means of grace because through them God evokes and sustains the faith that justifies. A right view of these things is possible only where there is a proper grasp of justification; so that, when justification falls, true knowledge of God's grace in human life falls with it. When Atlas loses his footing, everything that rests on his shoulders collapses too.

The Doctrine Analysed

A study of the expositions of justification in the works of the Reformers and the Church confessions produced under their leadership in Germany, France, Switzerland, the Low Countries, and Britain reveals such unanimity that the material may be generalised about as a single whole. The main points stressed are these:

1 The need of justification

The biblical frame of reference, within which alone justification can be understood and apart from which it remains, in the strictest sense, unintelligible, is created, said the Reformers, by two realities: human sin, which is universal, and divine judgment, which is inescapable. The basic fact is that the God who made us intends to take account of us, measuring us by his own standards, and from his imminent inquisition nothing can shield us. All stand naked and open before the searcher of hearts, and all must prepare to meet their God. But that being so, all hope is gone; for, being morally and spiritually perverse throughout, we are forced to recognise that in God's eyes we are hopelessly and helplessly guilty, justly subject to his condemning sentence and to that judicial rejection which the Bible calls his *wrath*. The pride which prompts us to rail at this

judgment as unjust is itself part of the perversity which makes
it just. Anyone who knows anything of his own inner corruption and of the holiness of his judge will find Luther's question,
'How may I find a gracious God?' rising in his heart unbidden
– but to this question the unaided human mind can find no
answer. To persons convicted of sin, efforts for self-
justification appear as the abortive products of self-ignorance;
those who have become realistic about themselves see clearly
that there is no road that way. Luther in the monastery sought
perfect *contritio* (sorrow for sin, out of love for God), without
which, so the theology of his day told him, there was no
forgiveness. No man ever worked harder than Luther to make
himself love God, but he could not do it. When, later, Luther
said that Romans was written to 'magnify sin',[3] what he meant
was that Romans aims to induce a realistic awareness of moral
and spiritual inability, and so create the self-despair which is
the anteroom of faith in Christ.

When the Reformers insisted that the Law must prepare for
the Gospel, this was what they meant. Conviction of sin,
springing from God-given self-knowledge, is, they said, a
necessary precondition for understanding justification, for it
alone makes faith possible. The Augsburg Confession of 1531
states: '. . . this whole doctrine [of justification] must be
related to the conflict of an alarmed conscience, and without
that conflict it cannot be grasped. So persons lacking this
experience, and profane men, are bad judges of this matter.'[4]
Calvin makes the same point in *Institutio* III.xii, a chapter on
the theme that justification must be studied in the solemnising
light of God's judgment-seat.[5] And John Owen preserves this
perspective when at the start of his classic treatise, *The
Doctrine of Justification by Faith* (1677), he writes:

The first inquiry . . . is after the proper relief of the conscience of a sinner pressed and perplexed with a sense of the
guilt of sin. For justification is the way and means, whereby
such a person doth obtain acceptance before God . . . And
nothing is pleadable in this cause, but what a man would
speak unto his own conscience in that state, or into the

conscience of another, when he is anxious under that inquiry.

And again:

> It is the practical direction of the consciences of men, in their application unto God by Jesus Christ, for deliverance from the curse due unto the apostate state, and peace with him, with the influence of the way thereof unto universal gospel obedience, that is alone to be designed in the handling of this doctrine. And therefore, unto him that would treat of it in a due manner, it is required that he . . . not dare to propose that unto others which he doth not abide by himself, in the most intimate recesses of his mind, under his nearest approaches unto God, in his surprisals with dangers, in deep afflictions, in his preparations for death, and most humble contemplations of the infinite distance between God and him. Other notions . . . not seasoned with these ingredients . . . are insipid and useless.[6]

Luther would have graduated Owen *summa cum laude* for that!

2   *The meaning of justification*

What justification is, said the Reformers, must be learned from Paul, its great New Testament expositor, who sees it clearly and precisely as a judicial act of God pardoning and forgiving our sins, accepting us as righteous, and instating us as his sons. Following Augustine, who studied the Bible in Latin and was partly misled by the fact that *justificare*, the Latin for Paul's δικαιοῦν, naturally means '*make* righteous', the Mediaevals had defined justification as pardon plus inner renewal, as the Council of Trent was also to do; but the Reformers saw that the Pauline meaning of δικαιοῦν is strictly forensic. So Calvin defines justification as 'acceptance, whereby God receives us into his favour and regards us as righteous; and we say that it consists in the remission of sins and the imputation of the righteousness of Christ.'[7] Justification is decisive for eternity, being in effect the judgment of the last day brought forward. Its source is God's grace, his initiative in free and sovereign love, and its ground is the merit and satisfaction – that is, the obedient sin-bearing death – of Jesus Christ, God's incarnate Son.[8]

Behind Calvin's phrase, 'the imputation of the righteousness of Christ', lies the characteristic 'Christ-and-his-people' Christology which was the centre of reference – the hub of the wheel, we might say – of the Reformers' entire doctrine of grace. The concern of this Christology, as of the New Testament Christology which moulded it, is soteriological, and its key thought is participation through exchange. This idea is spelled out as follows. The Son of God came down from heaven in order to bring us to share with him the glory to which he has now returned. By incarnation he entered into solidarity with us, becoming through his Father's appointment the last Adam, the second head of the race, acting on our behalf in relation to God. As man, he submitted to the great and decisive exchange set forth in 2 Corinthians 5:21: 'For our sake he [God] made him to be sin who knew no sin, so that in him we might become the righteousness of God.' 'This', said Luther, 'is that mystery which is rich in divine grace to sinners, wherein by a wonderful exchange our sins are no longer ours but Christ's, and the righteousness of Christ is not Christ's but ours. He has emptied himself of his righteousness that he might clothe us with it, and fill us with it; and he has taken our evils upon himself that he might deliver us from them. So that now the righteousness of Christ is ours not only objectively (as they term it) but formally also' – that is, it is not only an ontological reality, 'there' for our benefit in some general sense, but it actually imparts to us the 'form', i.e., the characteristic, of being righteous in God's sight.[9]

Our sins were reckoned (imputed) to Christ, so that he bore God's judgement on them, and in virtue of this his righteousness is reckoned ours, so that we are pardoned, accepted, and given a righteous man's status for his sake. Christians in themselves are sinners who never fully meet the Law's demands; nonetheless, says Luther, 'they are righteous because they believe in Christ, whose righteousness covers them and is imputed to them'.[10] On this basis, despite all the shortcomings of which they are conscious, believers may be sure of eternal salvation, and rejoice in hope of the glory of God. And this, said the Reformers, is what it means to know Christ; for we do not know him, however much else we may know about him, till we see him as Christ *pro nobis*, dying, rising, and reigning for us as our gracious Saviour.

The Reformers were explicit in grounding our justification on Christ's penal substitution for us under the punitive wrath of God. According to Anselm, whose view had been standard in the West for four centuries before the Reformers, Christ's death was a satisfaction for our sins offered to God as an alternative to the punishment of our persons. The Reformers assumed this formula, but added two emphases which went beyond Anselm – first, that the Son's offering was made at the Father's bidding; second, that Christ's death made satisfaction precisely by being the punishment of our sins in his person.[11] Satisfaction, in other words, was by substitution; vicarious sin-bearing by the Son of God is the ground of our justification and hope. In saying this, the Reformers were not offering a speculative rationale of Christ's work of reconciliation, but simply expounding and confessing the Scriptural reality of it. They did not discuss, as later generations were to do, why, or indeed whether, God must judge sin retributively as a basis of pardoning it, or how vicarious punishment can be shown to be meaningful and moral, or any of the other questions which the Socinian critique of the Reformed doctrine was to raise; their concern was just to enter fully into biblical thinking on this matter, and to relay it as clearly and precisely as possible. Luther, commenting on Galatians 3:13, 'Christ redeemed us from the curse of the law, having become a curse for us', states penal substitution like this:

We are sinners and thieves, and therefore guilty of death and everlasting damnation. But Christ took all our sins upon him, and for them died upon the cross . . . all the prophets did foresee in spirit, that Christ should become the greatest transgressor, murderer, adulterer, thief, rebel, blasphemer, etc., that ever was . . . for he being made a sacrifice, for the sins of the whole world, is now an innocent person and without sins . . . our most merciful Father, seeing us to be oppressed, overwhelmed with the curse of the law, and so to be holden under the same that we could never be delivered from it by our own power, sent his only Son into the world and laid upon him all the sins of all men, saying: Be thou Peter that denier; Paul that persecutor, blasphemer and cruel oppressor; David that adulterer; that sinner which did eat the apple in Paradise; that thief which hanged upon the cross; and, briefly, be thou the person which hath committed the sins of all men; see therefore that thou pay and satisfy for them. Here now cometh the law and saith: I find him a sinner, and that such a one as hath taken upon him the sins of all men, and I see no sins but in him; therefore let him die upon the cross. And so he setteth upon him and killeth him. By this means the whole world is purged and cleansed from all sins, and so delivered from death and all evils.[12]

Calvin speaks less vivid and dramatically, but to the same effect:

Because the curse caused by our guilt was awaiting us at God's heavenly judgment seat . . . Christ's condemnation before Pontius Pilate . . . is recorded, so that we might know that the penalty to which we were subject had been inflicted on this righteous man . . . when he was arraigned before a judgment-seat, accused and put under pressure by testimony, and sentenced to death by the words of a judge, we know by these records that this role was that of (*personam sustinuit*) a guilty wrongdoer . . . we see the role of the sinner and criminal represented in Christ, yet from his shining innocence it becomes obvious that he was burdened with the misdoing of others rather than his own . . . This is

our acquittal, that the guilt which exposed us to punishment
was transferred to the head of God's Son . . .

At every point he substituted himself in our place (*in vicem
nostram ubique se supposuerit*) to pay the price of our
redemption.[13]

This is the characteristic doctrine of the Reformation concerning the death of Christ. It was an act of obedient substitution on his part, an acceptance in his own person of the penalty
due to us, in virtue of which the holy judge declares guilty
sinners immune from punishment and righteous in his sight.
The great exchange is no legal fiction, no arbitrary pretence, no
mere word-game on God's part, but a costly achievement. The
divinely established solidarity between Christ and his people
was such that he was in truth 'made sin' for us, and 'bore in his
soul the dreadful torments of a condemned and lost man',[14] so
that in our souls the joy of knowing God's forgiveness and
favour might reign for ever. This, to the Reformers, was the
heart and height of the work of divine grace, not to be
wrangled over, but to be trusted and adored.

3   The means of justification

Justification, said the Reformers, is by faith *only*. Why so? Not
because there are no 'good works' in the believer's life (on the
contrary, faith works by love untiringly and the knowledge of
justification is the supreme ethical dynamic),[15] but because
Christ's vicarious righteousness is the *only* ground of justification, and it is *only* by faith that we lay hold of Christ, for his
righteousness to become ours. Faith is a conscious acknowledgment of our own unrighteousness and ungodliness
and on that basis a looking to Christ as our righteousness, a
clasping of him as the ring clasps the jewel (so Luther), a
receiving of him as an empty vessel receives treasure (so
Calvin), and a reverent, resolute reliance on the biblical promise of life through him for all who believe. Faith is our act, but
not our work; it is an instrument of reception without being a

means of merit; it is the work in us of the Holy Spirit, who both evokes it and through it ingrafts us into Christ in such a sense that we know at once the personal relationship of sinner to Saviour and disciple to Master and with that the dynamic relationship of resurrection life, communicated through the Spirit's indwelling. So faith takes, and rejoices, and hopes, and loves, and triumphs.

One of the unhealthiest features of Protestant theology today is its preoccupation with faith: faith, that is, viewed man-centredly as a state of existential commitment. Inevitably, this preoccupation diverts thought away from faith's object, even when this is clearly conceived – as too often in modern theology it is not. Though the Reformers said much about faith, even to the point of calling their message of justification 'the doctrine of faith', their interest was not of the modern kind. It was not subject-centred but object-centred, not psychological but theological, not anthropocentric but Christocentric. The Reformers saw faith as a relationship, not to oneself, as did Tillich, but to the living Christ of the Bible, and they fed faith in themselves and in others by concentrating on that Christ as the Saviour and Lord by whom our whole life must be determined. A. M. Stibbs echoed the Reformers' 'object-centred' account of faith with precision when he wrote:

The faith of the individual must be seen as having no value in itself, but as discovering value wholly and solely through movement towards and committal to Christ. It must be seen as simply a means of finding all one's hope outside oneself in the person and work of another; and not in any sense an originating cause or objective ground of justification. For true faith is active only in the man who is wholly occupied with Christ; its practice means that every blessing is received from another. For this reason faith is exclusive and intolerant of company; it is only truly present when any and every contribution towards his salvation on the part of the believer or on the part of the Church is absolutely and unequivocally shut out. Justification must be seen and received as a blessing dependent wholly and exclusively on Christ alone, on what he is and what he has done – a blessing enjoyed simply through being joined directly to him, through finding one's all in him, through drawing one's all from him, without the interposition of any other mediator or mediating channel whatever.[16]

The Doctrine Distorted

To the Reformers' doctrine of justification by faith alone Reformed theology has held down the centuries, maintaining it to be both Scriptural in substance and life-giving in effect.[17] This tenacity has, however, involved constant conflict, as it still does. Two things have long threatened the truth as stated: first, the intruding of works as the ground of justification; second, the displacing of the cross as the ground of justification. Both are familiar weeds in the Church's garden; both express in very obvious ways the craving for self-justification which lurks (often in disguise!) in the fallen human heart. Something may be said about each.

First, *the intruding of works*. This happens the moment we look to anything in ourselves, whether of nature or of grace, whether to acts of faith or to deeds of repentance, as a basis for pardon and acceptance. Reformed theology had to fight this tendency in both Romanism and Arminianism. The Council of Trent (1547, Session VI) defined justification as inner renewal plus pardon and acceptance, the renewal being the basis of the pardon, and went on to affirm that the 'sole formal cause' (*unica formalis causa*) of justification, in both its aspects, was God's righteousness imparted through baptism as its instrumental cause.[18] 'Formal cause' means that which gives a thing its quality; so the thesis is that the ground of our being pardoned and accepted by infused grace is our having been made genuinely righteous in ourselves. (This links up with the Roman idea that 'concupiscence' in the regenerate is not sin till it is yielded to.[19]) In reply, a host of Reformed divines, continental and British, episcopal and non-episcopal, drew out at length the Reformers' contention, discussed above, that the 'sole formal cause' of justification is not God's righteousness imparted, but Christ's righteousness imputed. The same point was pressed against the seventeenth-century Arminians, who held that faith is 'counted for righteousness' because it is in itself actual personal righteousness, being obedience to the Gospel viewed as God's new Law, and being also an act of self-determination that is in no sense determined by God. The argument against both Romans and Arminians was that by finding the ground of justification in the believer himself they contradicted the Scriptures, nourished pride, and a spirit of self-sufficiency and self-reliance in religion, so encouraging self-ignorance, destroyed assurance by making final salvation depend upon ourselves rather than on God, obscured the nature of faith as self-renouncing trust, and robbed both God's grace and God's Son of the full glory that was their due. It is not enough, declared the Reformed writers, to say that without Christ our justification could not be; one must go on to say that it is on the ground of his obedience as our substitutionary sin-bearer, and that alone, that righteousness is reckoned to us, and sin cancelled. The Westminster Confession (XI.i) has both Romanism and Arminianism in its eye when it declares, with classic precision and balance:

> Those whom God effectually calleth he also freely justifieth; not by infusing righteousness into them, but by pardoning their sins, and by accounting and accepting their persons as righteous; not for anything wrought in them, or done by them, but for Christ's sake alone; not by imputing faith itself, the act of believing, or any other evangelical obedience, to them as their righteousness; but by imputing the obedience and satisfaction of Christ unto them, they receiving and resting on him and his righteousness by faith; which faith they have not of themselves; it is the gift of God.

Second, *the displacing of the cross* as the ground of justification. This happens when the correlation between Christ's sin-bearing and our pardon is lost sight of. It can occur, and has occurred, in various ways. The truth of biblical teaching may be queried, in which case one may say (for instance) that though judicial notions meant much to Paul, because of his rabbinic conditioning, and to the Reformers, in whose culture legal concepts were dominant, they are really unfit for expressing God's forgiveness, and the idea that our heavenly Father's pardon had to be paid for by the blood of Christ is in any case monstrous. Or the objective reality of God's wrath against sin may be specifically denied, and the cross be construed in terms other than penal substitution. But in every case where the correlation breaks, the effect is to shut us up to supposing that God, after all, pardons and accepts us for something in ourselves – our repentance, or the righteousness of which it is the promise. So we return by a new route to the idea that the ground of justification is, after all, our own works, actual or potential. The history of the older rationalism and liberalism over two centuries shows many instances of this.

A third disruptive notion, more recently launched, is *the eliminating of faith* as the means of justification. This happens in universalism, which affirms that through God's love in creation and redemption all men have been redeemed and justified already, and the only question is whether they yet know it. So justification is before faith and apart from it, and faith is no more than discovery of this fact. Clearly, neither on this view nor on those noted in the two previous paragraphs can faith be given its biblical significance as the means whereby a sinner lays hold of Christ, and from being under wrath comes to be under grace.

Justification by faith only, as Reformed Christians know, is a 'Gospel mystery', a revealed secret of God which is a wonder of grace, transcending human wisdom and indeed contradicting it. No wonder, then, if again and again, it is misunderstood, or objected to, or twisted out of shape! But, as we have seen, to those who know anything of God's holiness and their own sinfulness the doctrine is in truth a lifeline and a doxology, a paean of praise and a song of triumph – as it was to the judicious Richard Hooker, with whose majestic and poignant declaration of it we close this section.

Christ hath merited righteousness for as many as are found
in him. In him God findeth us, if we be faithful; for by faith
we are incorporated into him. Then, although in ourselves
we be altogether sinful and unrighteous, yet even the man
who in himself is impious, full of iniquity, full of sin; him
being found in Christ by faith, and having his sin in hatred
through repentance; him God beholdeth with a gracious
eye, putteth away his sin by not imputing it, taketh quite
away the punishment due thereto, by pardoning it; and
accepteth him in Jesus Christ, as perfectly righteous, as if he
had fulfilled all that is commanded him in the law: shall I
say, more perfectly righteous than if himself had fulfilled the
whole law? I must take heed what I say; but the Apostle
saith, 'God made him which knew no sin, to be sin for us;
that we might be made the righteousness of God in him.'
Such we are in the sight of God the Father, as is the very Son
of God himself. Let it be counted folly, or phrensy, or fury,
or whatsoever. It is our wisdom, and our comfort; we care
for no knowledge in the world but this, that man hath
sinned, and God hath suffered; that God hath made himself
the sin of men, and that men are made the righteousness of
God.[20]

The Reformed Doctrine in the Church of England[21]

Had the post-Reformation Church of England held to
Hooker's view of justification, there would today be no uncertainty as to whether Anglican soteriology is Reformed or not.
What actually happened, however, has created much uncertainty at this point. The convulsions of the mid-seventeenth
century threw up a generation of teachers whose views embo-
died the first two of the distortions described above, while the
past century and a half has seen Anglican theologians exploring the third. The Reformed and evangelical status of the
Church of England has often been called in question by reason
of ideas about ministry and sacraments that have surfaced
within it, but a profounder reason for the query would be the

un-Reformed notions about justification on which these views rest.

To be more specific: under Dutch Arminian and Greek patristic influence, and with the laudable purpose of highlighting the need for holiness as the path to final salvation, men like William Forbes, Henry Hammond, Jeremy Taylor, Herbert Thorndike and George Bull reacted against the position spelt out by Hooker and upheld during the century after him as both biblical and officially Anglican by, for instance, Bishops George Downame (Downham), Lancelot Andrewes, John Davenant, Joseph Hall, James Ussher and Thomas Barlow, those Anglicans who framed the Irish Articles (1615) and the Westminster Confession (1647), and theologians William Perkins, William Whitaker, John Donne, John Bramhall, Robert Sanderson, William Beveridge, and the great Independent John Owen. Reaction took these later Carolines in different directions on points of detail, but in their goal of seeking an accommodation of, or a *via media* between, Protestant and Tridentine positions without transgressing the Anglican formularies they were at one, and the same theological perspectives appear in them all, as follows:

First, they accepted the Socinian contention that the Reformed doctrine of Christ's righteousness imputed to believers is logically antinomian in the sense that it makes personal holiness unnecessary and irrelevant for final salvation. Recoiling from the bogy of antinomianism, they sought to show that personal holiness is the direct ground of God's acceptance of the Christian at the last.

Second, they accepted the Arminian idea that God's new covenant proclaimed in the Gospel is essentially a conditional promise, based on Christ's death as its presupposition, to give pardon and life in heaven to those who practise repentance and faith to the very end. Repentance and faith thus constitute their personal righteousness, and are the ground of God's award.

Third, they accepted the Tridentine teaching that sinful impulse (concupiscence) is not a guilty thing in God's sight till it is yielded to, and that a grace-aided sinner is capable of unflawed acts of faith, repentance and obedience which he himself may properly regard as his own righteousness, just as, according to this teaching, God does.

Fourth, they accepted the redefinition of faith which Arminians and some Puritans had come up with, according to which faith is essentially volitional (active) rather than intellectual (passive), as the Reformers had conceived it to be. Instead of being a God-given certainty of one's acceptance here and now for Jesus' sake, faith thus became a resolute commitment to obey Christ; instead of being a fiducial reception through the Spirit of a divine assurance, based on God's promise in Scripture, that one is this moment and for ever justified in Christ, it became in effect a meritorious work whereby justification is sought; instead of being the root of repentance, it became indistinguishable from repentance, so that it could now actually be equated with one's 'new obedience' in Christ.

The effect was to disrupt the correlation between Christ's obedience to death and our present justification, and to make justification by faith appear as a new form of justification by works, the difference from the old form being simply that less is now asked for as a condition of justification than was formerly the case. Once, perfect obedience to the law was required; now, a sustained act of faith will do the trick. 'Our Saviour hath brought down the market', wrote Henry Hammond.[22] But this is not the Reformed doctrine, even though it is sometimes heard today on evangelical lips. The nature of faith in its relation to God's own justifying word needs more study among evangelical Christians than it commonly receives.

As a result of the Caroline heritage, variously adapted, taking a permanent place in the Anglican mix, and prompting a persistent critique of *sola fide* teaching as if it means that one is justified through feeling justified (!), Anglican thinking about justification is today in a state of some confusion. Space forbids further discussion of its cross-currents here; suffice it to say two things only. First, the foundation of the Reformed doctrine is belief in the total inability of fallen man ('those who are in the flesh cannot please God' (Rom. 8:8)), particularity of Christ's redemption ('who loved me and gave himself for me'

(Gal. 2:20)), and the sovereign mercy of God in effectual calling ('those whom he called he also justified' (Rom. 8:30)), and it cannot be stated in any other context or frame of reference. Second, assurance of final salvation is integral to the Reformed doctrine of God's justifying gift in Christ, and this is something which no form of semi-Pelagianism, whether Protestant (Arminian) or Roman Catholic (Tridentine), can accept. It is greatly to be hoped that the Reformed doctrine will reassert itself within Anglicanism in these days, and that when ARCIC II takes up the subject of justification it will be the Reformed doctrine that is laid on the table in the Anglican name.

5

JUSTIFICATION AND THE EASTERN ORTHODOX CHURCHES

Gerald Bray

The inclusion of a chapter on Eastern Orthodox theology in a symposium on justification by faith must surely be an unprecedented event. Those not familiar with the Eastern Church may feel that this customary neglect is unjustified and that the riches of Eastern theology might reveal aspects of the doctrine which have been overlooked in the West. Others, perhaps with a greater knowledge of the subject, will be surprised to find justification by faith mentioned at all in the context of Eastern theology. They will urge that not only the historical debate but the very concept itself depends on a Western and especially Augustinian framework which has never been understood, much less accepted, in the East.

At first sight, the second view is undoubtedly safer than the first, especially as the Eastern Church has never experienced anything even remotely like the Reformation in Western Europe. But true though this is, it is also true that Eastern theology has had to deal in its own way with the substance of the issues raised by the Western debate, and offers an interesting contrast to our own way of thinking about the subject. At a time when the fundamental issues of theology are being reassessed on a wider scale, it will help us if we take a fresh look at a very different approach to the whole subject, and ask ourselves whether we have gone the right way in history, or whether it would have been better for us to have followed this very different road.

Sin and Righteousness in Orthodox Thought

The development of Eastern theology cannot be properly understood without some reference to its roots in a characteristically Greek way of thinking. The Greeks conceived of the universe in terms of *natures* or *substances* which expressed themselves in the form of individual entities. Each individual item was called a *hypostasis*, a word corresponding to the later Latin use of *subsistentia* and *persona*. The early fathers of the church shared this basic outlook for many centuries, but eventually it became apparent that the logic of the Christian revelation must push them in a different direction. The admission that God was tripersonal raised the notion of the *hypostasis*, hitherto logically dependent on that of *nature*, to a position of controlling authority. In the incarnation of Christ, it was the person of the Word who united a human nature to himself, thereby revolutionising the traditional understanding of the relationship between person (*hypostasis*) and nature.

This new piece of thinking, which was canonised in the famous Definition of the Person of Christ at the Council of Chalcedon in 451, was common to both Eastern and Western Christianity. For about a century afterwards, both traditions moved along roughly parallel lines, but by the seventh century differences of emphasis could no longer be concealed. The East knew little or nothing of Augustine, whose thought was increasingly dominant in the West, and was beginning to develop its own specifically Byzantine theology, which interpreted the traditional dogmas along rather different lines from those which the West had embraced.

The primacy of the divine person over the human nature in Christ was applied by analogy to the rest of mankind as well. Human persons were held to derive their being from their participation in the divine reason (logos) which was the image of God in man, and was radically distinguished from human nature. Sin entered the word because the mind of man had been beguiled by Satan, who was jealous of the special relationship which man was destined to have with God. The sin of Adam was a personal act of his own free will that deprived him of the means of fulfilling his destiny, which was to overcome, by virtue of his personal relationship with the logos, the mortality of his human nature. Satan by his trickery gave death its fundamentally unnatural and unjust rule over mankind.

According to this way of thinking, original sin is the bondage of the human race to death. It is not an aspect of human nature, which merely obeys its own inherent law of mortality, but an expression of personal choice. As such, it is not transmitted by natural means from one generation to the next, but re-emerges afresh in each child of Adam. No one inherits the guilt of his ancestors; each man or woman is responsible only for the acts of his own free will.

To the Western mind, this scheme raises one obvious difficulty. If sin is a purely individual affair, why is it universal? Does the sin of Adam have no bearing on us? To this, Eastern theology replies that the link must be sought in the concept of death. The sin of Adam introduced the reign of death into the world, and it is this evil dominion which now causes all men to sin. The proof of this is found in Romans 5:12, the famous verse which has been so hotly debated in Western theology. The verse reads: *di'henos anthrōpou he hamartia eis ton kosmon eisēlthen kai dia tēi hamartiāi ho thanatos eph hōi pantes hēmarton.*

The classical Greek interpretation of this is: *by one man sin came into the world, and by sin death, because of which all have sinned.* The last clause is made to depend directly on *death*, a view which is seldom accepted in the West.[1] The classical Eastern position, with its variations, is expressed by John Meyendorff as follows:

> There is indeed a consensus in Greek patristic and Byzantine traditions in identifying the inheritance of the Fall as an inheritance essentially of mortality rather than of sinfulness, sinfulness being merely a consequence of mortality. The idea appears in Chrysostom, who specifically denies the imputation of sin to the descendants of Adam; in the eleventh-century commentator Theophylact of Ochrida; and in later Byzantine authors, particularly Gregory Palamas. The

always-more-sophisticated Maximus the Confessor, when he speaks of the consequences of the sin of Adam, identifies them mainly with the mind's submission to the flesh and finds in sexual procreation the most obvious expression of man's acquiescence in animal instincts; but as we have seen, sin remains, for Maximus, a personal act, and inherited guilt is impossible for him, as for the others. The wrong choice made by Adam brought in passion, corruption, and mortality, but not inherited guilt.[2]

From this it can be seen that a fundamentally different understanding of the Incarnation and the Atonement from that of the West is required by the logic of Eastern theology. East and West agree that the Crucifixion was the purpose of the Incarnation, but not that the latter need never have taken place had mankind not fallen into sin. The goal of human life was the perfection of human nature, and the Incarnation was an essential precondition of this, regardless of sin.[3] The cross was made necessary by sin, but not to vanquish it by exacting a just retribution in the punishment of the only one worthy to make the sacrifice. The point of the cross was to vanquish *death*, thereby making it possible for man to return to the state of Adam and renew his progress towards deification, secure in the knowledge that Christ had gone before, and that he had sent the Holy Spirit, who in the life-giving 'drug' (*pharmakon*) of the sacrament applies Christ's victory to the Church.

By now it will be obvious that the Eastern Church has no room in its theology for a doctrine of justification because it has no room for a doctrine of original sin which imputes Adam's guilt to the whole human race. Meyendorff states categorically that 'Byzantine theology did not produce any significant elaboration of the Pauline doctrine of justification expressed in Romans and Galatians.'[4] It is possible that in the third century Origen (*c.* 185–254) was the first to gloss 'by faith *alone*' in Romans 3:28, thereby bringing out the sharp contrast with works which we normally associate with Luther.[5] It is also a fact that Theodore of Mopsuestia, another great Biblical scholar of antiquity, made explicit reference to justification by faith in his commentary on this verse. On the other hand neither of these writers is entirely orthodox, and their writings cannot be taken as typical of the Eastern tradition.

In so far as justification was understood at all, it was assimilated to sanctification and the final re-creation of all things in Christ. The theologians did not envisage any point of crisis in the life of the believer when he came to the conscious knowledge that by faith in the finished work of Christ his sin and guilt had been taken away. Rather the Christian was involved in a continuing process of renewal, greatly accelerated by the Incarnation and by the works of the incarnate Lord, but still far from finished. In this context the superiority of Christianity (*faith*) over Judaism (*law*) lay in the superiority of the righteousness which it made attainable. The righteousness of the Christian was to exceed the righteousness of the Scribes and Pharisees in degree more than in kind, and a life of good works was a necessary aid to final salvation. That did not mean that these works were not also the fruit of grace, however. It was the sacrament of baptism, bringing to the individual the liberating and life-giving power of the risen Christ, which made a life of good works possible. Without baptism, there could be no righteousness at all, and the 'good works' of the heathen were a delusion.

From this it will be apparent that Eastern theology has room for a doctrine of righteousness by faith, provided that the latter is understood as God-given belief in divine realities and made objective in the grace given at baptism and confirmed in the other sacraments. At the same time it is improper to speak of justification in the Western sense, because there is not the same idea of guilt deriving from original sin.

Orthodoxy and the Reformation

When we turn to the historical debate, we can see how the fundamental outlook of the East was bound to be unsympathetic to the Reformers. Already in the ninth century the patriarch Photius had launched a full-scale attack on Western theology, condemning its most characteristically Augustinian emphases, and not least Augustine's doctrine of original sin.[6] The position in the sixteenth century and since has remained virtually the same, though there have been attempts to reach some kind of mutual understanding.

The initiative in ecumenical dialogue with Eastern Orthodoxy has almost invariably come from outside. This is partly because the Eastern Churches regard themselves as the norm from which others have departed and partly because, for most of the modern period, they have been subject to political and spiritual harassment, which has inhibited them from any free expression of their views. At the time of the Reformation, the Greek Church was living in the shadow of the Islamic Turks, who threatened to engulf Western Europe as well. Only Russia had managed to preserve its freedom, but its theological tradition was as yet undeveloped and the country was still barely emerging from barbarism.

Martin Luther and his contemporaries were not able to consult the Greeks directly about the Reformation, and Luther's own views on their Church were rudimentary. On the one hand, he believed that they were not schismatics because of their refusal to acknowledge the Pope, but on the other hand, he saw the Turks as a justly-deserved scourge for their sins and corruption. A few of his followers tried to make contact with Constantinople, but without much success, and Luther must have sensed that any move in that direction would prove a disappointment. Towards the end of his life, Melanchthon decided to try again, and a Greek translation of the Augsburg Confession was dispatched to Constantinople by the hand of a Greek who had been converted to Lutheranism. The Confession proved such an embarrassment to the Greeks, who saw the Lutherans as potential friends and allies against the far more dangerous Roman Catholics, that the patriarch diplomatically mislaid the letter and made no reply.[7]

That was in 1553. Shortly after that a renegade Greek managed to win some support for a Lutheran state in Moldavia, but his attempts to reform the Orthodox Church from within were a disastrous failure and gave rise to suspicions in Constantinople which did not help the cause of ecumenism. Another attempt at getting a Greek assessment of the Augsburg Confession was made in 1574 when a group of professors from Tübingen once more approached the patriarch. The Greek hierarchy was as embarrassed as it had been in 1559, but the presence of Lutheran ambassadors in Constantinople made the earlier tactics impossible and after much hesitation the patriarch, Jeremias II, replied in full on May 15th, 1576.[8] In this letter, he took each point of the Confession and gave a detailed answer. Other correspondence was to follow (it was eventually broken off in 1581), but the first letter has acquired the status of an official doctrinal statement, and is the closest an official Orthodox body has come to making a direct pronouncement on the doctrine of justification by faith.

The patriarch replied to the Confession point by point, with a special paragraph on original sin followed by sections on justifying faith, the ministry of the Word and good works. On the first point, the patriarch expresses full agreement with the Confession on what could easily have been the thorny issue of original sin. The reason for this is almost certainly the fact that the Confession makes no direct reference to inherited guilt. That doctrine is implicit in the Confession's reference to the Pelagians, and would certainly have been assumed in Roman Catholic circles, so the omission can hardly have been intentional. Nor is it likely that the Lutherans were aware of Orthodox misgivings on the point. It must, therefore, be concluded that agreement was, in this case, the result of ignorance and misunderstanding.

The next chapter deals specifically with justifying faith, and here the patriarch states frankly that, in his opinion, the Reformers have erred. 'The Catholic Church', says Jeremias, 'requires living faith, which is manifested by good works', and in support of this he quotes James 2:17, a passage which the Lutherans found particularly difficult to interpret. He also quotes a passage from Basil of Caesarea which states that heavenly grace is given as an ally to human effort (*spoudē*), and will not enter anyone who is not trying to live a good life. He also applies Matthew 18:19 in such a way that the soul of man and the Spirit of God are supposed to unite in petition to God, a combination which is necessary in order to prove effective. Worthy repentance demands an active hatred of evil on the part of the one seeking it, and this hatred must be evidenced in a life of good works.

Naturally, Jeremias is aware of human weakness, and he does not think of a life of good works as being performed without divine aid. On the contrary, God has promised, out of his love for man, to give him all the help he needs. This is the meaning of Isaiah 49:8, quoted by Paul in 2 Corinthians 6:2: 'In a time of favour I have answered you, in a day of salvation I have helped you.' The auxiliary role of divine grace in the work of justification could hardly be more apparent.

One of the striking features about these chapters in Jeremias' letter is the extent to which they rely on Scripture to buttress the argument. The familiar distribution of biblical and patristic quotations in roughly equal proportions has been distorted quite drastically in favour of the former. Moreover, as Jeremias warms to his theme, particularly in the section on good works, the biblical texts multiply, and references to patristic sources almost vanish from sight. Is there anything to explain this rather curious fact?

It is necessary at this point to speculate what Orthodox and Lutherans may have known of each other independently of the Augsburg Confession and the correspondence it provoked. Did Jeremias realise, for example, that Luther held to a doctrine of *sola Scriptura* and answer on that basis, rather as Tertullian answered Marcion, to prove that even so he was still wrong? Yet the Greeks would not have learned this from the Confession itself, nor from the covering letter, which specifically invoked the authority of the seven Ecumenical Councils. Of course it is not impossible that Jeremias chose to answer in the way he did out of respect for the traditions of the Greek fathers whose views he was concerned to uphold, but the almost complete absence of patristic quotations seems too anachronistic at this date to be wholly coincidental.

As for Lutheran knowledge of Orthodoxy, we have already

seen that there are good reasons to suspect it of having been minimal. But Jaroslav Pelikan has recently pointed out that the Greek translation of the Augsburg Confession, which he mistakenly ascribes to Melanchthon,[9] differs in certain particulars from its Latin prototype, and he attributes the discrepancies to a sensitivity to the Eastern tradition on the part of the translator.[10] On the subject of justification, Pelikan records the fact that the Latin verb *iustificari* is translated *hagiazesthai*, 'to be sanctified', a modification which he states was made in order to interpret to Greek minds 'the doctrine of justification by grace through faith, without the works of sanctification'.[11] If so, it was a remarkably clumsy way of doing it, since it was bound to suggest what Jeremias evidently took it to mean, viz. that good works had no place at all in the Christian life.

It is quite true that it was not easy to render the Western teaching into Greek, despite the existence of such words as *dikaiōsis* (justification) and *dikaiousthai* (justify). The expression *pistis dikaiōtikē* (justifying faith) has the air of a neologism[12] and must have sounded odd to Greek ears. But the very existence of the phrase argues against the use of *hagiazesthai* as a substitute. It is much more probable that the translator, failing to perceive the crucial difference between justification and sanctification (probably on the assumption that one led to the other anyway), forgot himself and made a peculiarly unfortunate mistake. If this is right, then his use of *hagiazesthai* is evidence not that he knew the Greek tradition and bent over backwards to accommodate it, but that he had no idea what a great misunderstanding would result from this error, and therefore his work displays ignorance of the subtleties of Greek theological thought. Certainly the lengthy reaction of Jeremias, who also fails to distinguish the two concepts, bears this out, as does what we know about the general state of Byzantine studies in Germany at that time.

The Seventeenth Century: Cyril I Lucaris and After

The correspondence between Jeremias and the professors of Tübingen might have been the end of the matter had not a most extraordinary event occurred some fifty years later, which reopened the whole question. Everyone, Orthodox and non-Orthodox alike, agrees that the most gifted man to occupy the patriarchal throne under the Turks was Cyril I Lucaris, who reigned from 1620 to 1635 and again from 1637 to 1638, when he was arrested and strangled by the Turks, partly at the instigation of his rival, Cyril II Contaris, who had been patriarch in the interval and was practically a pensioner of the Jesuits. Cyril I had studied in the West and made many Protestant friends. He was accused by his opponents of being a Lutheran, but it was to Calvin that he was chiefly attracted, and it is as a Calvinist that he has subsequently been known.

Cyril's new views saw the light of day in his *Eastern Confession of the Christian Faith*, which appeared in Latin at Geneva in 1629. The Greek manuscript in Cyril's own hand dates from 1631, when it too was published. This document marks a historic turning-point in the relations between the Eastern Church and the Protestant West. In formal terms, it is a surrender to the Western method of practising theology. The mystical traditions of the East had always fought shy of making dogmatic statements, and not since John of Damascus (*c.* 675–749) had anything like a compendium of doctrine appeared. Cyril's action provoked a series of replies in similar style, culminating in the Confession of Dositheus, Patriarch of Jerusalem, which was adopted by a synod held in that city in 1672. Between the dates of the two Confessions, the Orthodox Church had finally faced up to, come to terms with and rejected the theology of the Reformation.

From the Protestant point of view, Cyril's Confession was a remarkable triumph. While he was careful not to deny the most cherished tenets of Eastern tradition, and apparently always believed in such things as the perpetual virginity of Mary, he made a number of concessions to Protestant thought which went against the spirit, if not the letter, of his Church's teaching. Cyril upheld the principle of *sola Scriptura* even to the point of admitting that the Church could err, and his doctrine of justification by faith is likewise fully Protestant in tone. In his own words: 'We believe that man is justified by faith, not by works. But when we say "by faith", we understand the correlative of faith, namely, the righteousness of Christ, which faith, performing the function of a hand, grasps and applies to us for salvation.'[13]

Good works, in this scheme of things, were 'testimonies of our faith and a confirmation of our calling', but they were inadequate to save man.[14]

Cyril's teaching on justification marks a considerable advance on the understanding of Jeremias fifty years earlier. Cyril distinguishes clearly between justification and sanctification, and manages to find a place for works under the latter heading. Given a little tact on his part and sympathy from his audience, he might have won over the Orthodox, at least part of the way. Unfortunately for him, neither quality was much in evidence. Cyril himself had chosen to attack the cult of icons in his Confession, a point which the Lutherans had wisely avoided bringing up with Jeremias II. This stung the opposition more than anything else, and in September 1638, two months after his death, he was anathematised as a wicked iconoclast by a synod held at Constantinople. Later there was a more thorough examination of his teachings by men not unsympathetic to Cyril as an individual, and after much argument the Confession was dissected and judgment pronounced on each clause in 1642. Needless to say, the section on justification was among those to be condemned.

There the matter might have rested, had it not been for the activity of a Russian ecclesiastic whose declared aim was to check the controversies aroused by Cyril and preserve the Orthodox population of the Western Ukraine from the inroads of Rome. Peter Moghila, though he was Metropolitan of Kiev, was in fact a Moldavian (Romanian) educated in the West. He therefore knew Latin, of which his native dialect was a descendant, much better than Greek, and wrote his *Orthodox Confession of the Faith* in that language at some time in

the 1630s. Not surprisingly, this document breathes a Western, though this time Roman Catholic air, which to the purer
Orthodox was almost as repugnant as Cyril's Calvinism.
Moghila's work suffered accordingly from a certain amount of
diplomatic emendation when it was translated into Greek in
1642, but even so it received only qualified approval at
Constantinople, despite its reception, in the emended form, at
the Synod of Iaşi (Jassy) in 1643.

On the subject of justification by faith, Moghila's Confession is remarkable in that it repeats almost verbatim the
doctrine enunciated by Jeremias II. There is, however, one
interesting addition which reveals the Latin influence. At the
end of his statement Moghila adds: 'They sin who hope to be
saved by faith alone, without good works.'[15] Disapproval had
become open condemnation, and the distinction between justification and sanctification had once more been lost from view.

The position adopted by Moghila was not substantially
altered by Dositheus, who in 1672 authorised for publication a
Confession which was actually composed, in the main, by the
Patriarch of Constantinople with the help of three of his
predecessors.[16] This document endeavours to modify the
Latin flavour of Moghila's Confession, but is just as firm in
negating the doctrine of justification by faith. The Confession
of Dositheus, being more in tune with traditional Eastern
patterns of thought, had a readier reception than that of Peter
Moghila and is now generally reckoned among the authoritative statements of Orthodox belief.[17] In another way, it also
represents the end of serious thinking in the Eastern Church
about the doctrine of justification. Not until the twentieth
century, when there was a wholly new departure in Orthodox
thought, do we find anything of comparable quality which
deals directly with this issue.

The Renewal of Orthodoxy: Vladimir Lossky

The cardinal event in the theological renewal of Orthodoxy in
our time was the Russian revolution of 1917. The replacement

of Orthodoxy by Marxism as the official ideology of Russia was interpreted by many Orthodox theologians as the inevitable and, of course, disastrous result of the progressive Westernisation of Russian society since the eighteenth century. Orthodoxy, which should have been the bulwark of the nation's true identity, had been compromised (it was said) by its own flirtations with the West even earlier. The whole period from Jeremias II to Dositheus came under review as the age in which the East had done little more than pick its way through the intricacies of essentially alien theological debates, ending up with a semi-Roman dogmatic system, uneasily – many would say, incongruously – grafted on to a very different tradition.

The Russian exiles who gathered in Paris between the wars saw a need to re-establish the foundations of Orthodox theology which had been allowed to decay over the years. Of course, they were not all of one mind, and the antipathy between Sergei Bulgakov (1871–1944) and Vladimir Lossky (1903–58) in particular became a legend. Now, a generation later, it is possible to look again at this movement and make some attempt to assess it. Of the two types of thought represented above, it is Lossky's which has so far proved the more influential, at least within Orthodoxy itself. Lossky sought to revive the more ancient, Byzantine traditions of his Church, of which he regarded the fourteenth-century Archbishop of Thessalonica, Gregory Palamas (1296–1359) as the supreme exponent. According to Lossky, Palamas developed a system of thought based on the mystical traditions of the Eastern Church, which was in effect an Eastern antidote to Augustine and Thomas Aquinas. In response to the neo-Thomism of the Catholics and the neo-Augustinianism (tempered, as appropriate, by neo-Lutheranism and neo-Calvinism) of the Protestants, Lossky proposed a kind of neo-Palamism which offered a way of escape from the dilemmas of the other two systems.[18]

A key plank in Lossky's system was the doctrine that man was created in the image and likeness of God. This is the glory of man, and corresponds to what we have learned to call his personhood. In making this point so clearly, Lossky was drawing on, rather than repeating, the theology of the Greek fathers, who were inclined to identify the image with the soul or with the mind (reason) of man. In fact it is a very Western idea, not uninfluenced by the personalism so widespread in French philosophical circles between the wars.

As a result of this emphasis, Lossky rejuvenated patristic ideas of original sin and salvation, which we have already mentioned. His short introduction to Orthodox theology contains a whole chapter on original sin, but nothing at all on justification, which does not fit into his scheme. The closest he comes to it is in his section on redemption, where he writes:

> Christ does not execute justice; He manifests it: He manifests that which God expects from the creature, the fullness [sic] of humanity, 'the maximum man' to take up the expression of Nicholas of Cusa. He fulfils the vocation of man betrayed by Adam: to live, and to nourish the universe, only from God. Such is God's justice. The Son, identical with God in His divine nature, acquires through the Incarnation the possibility of fulfilling it. For He can then submit to the Father as if He were distant from Him, renounce this will of His own given Him by His humanity, and give Himself totally, even unto death, that the Father may be glorified. God's justice is that man should be no longer separated from God. It is the restoration of humanity in Christ, the true Adam.[19]

Thus understood, the life and death of Christ are the perfect example for us to follow in the pursuit of our own salvation. Justification and sanctification are both relegated to the sidelines by an even greater concept − the idea of deification (*theōsis*) by which man's nature is transformed from mortality to immortality. Faith, good works and the means of grace co-operate in bringing about this cosmic transformation of the human being.

It cannot be stressed too highly that Lossky's brilliant reinterpretation of the Eastern tradition, while it has not driven out its rivals completely, has come to influence an ever-widening circle of Orthodox thinkers. Its details will undoubtedly continue to be worked out, and its extreme anti-Westernism will probably in the end be modified to some extent, but his grasp of the tradition is such that his place in Orthodox theology appears secure. What comment can a Western writer make, especially with regard to the concept of justification? Must we accept as valid a theological system which has no place for it and carry on accordingly?

The Problem of Original Sin

Any critique of Eastern thought, particularly as this is represented by Lossky and his disciples, must begin with the doctrine of original sin. This, as we have already noted, is seen as an operation of Adam's free-will, with consequences for human nature which is now subject to mortality. Insofar as all men are mortal, original sin is universal, but there is no idea of inherited guilt. Guilt is acquired by each individual, exercising his personal free-will in the direction of sin. At the same time, however, man can use his free-will to seek salvation, and in doing so receives the grace of God, dispensed in various ways, which leads him to immortality.

The first difficulty with this is the place of the *will*. If Adam sinned by an act of the will and this sin brought human nature into bondage, how can man now possess free-will? The Second Council of Constantinople in 681, by condemning Monotheletism, condemned the idea that Christ's will inhered in his person as such. Christ was declared to have two wills, which meant that each will was conceived as belonging to, indeed as an element in, a nature, human in one case, divine in the other. If this doctrine is applied consistently to anthropology, it will be concluded immediately that the will is in bondage to sin along with the rest of human nature. Orthodox theology has failed to make this equation, and therefore it can speak of a fallen human being exercising free-will. But this is a theological oversight.

The second difficulty concerns the concept of *mortality*. The

Bible states categorically that 'the wages of sin is death' (Rom. 6:23). This has been objectified by the Orthodox to mean that Adam's sin is the cause of mortality. But a careful reading of Genesis 1–3 will reveal that this interpretation is incorrect. Adam was created *mortal* (cf Gen. 3:22), but on the understanding that his obedience would preserve him from *death* (Gen. 2:17). A distinction must be drawn here which the Orthodox have not made. Nor is it legitimate to appeal to Romans 5:12 in defence of the view that mortality is the cause of sin. This is a controversial passage with many possible interpretations, but the most natural exegesis surely is that which takes *eph' hōi* to refer to the whole of the preceding (*hōi* being read as an inclusive neuter).[20] Sin thus derives from Adam's act of disobedience directly, not from the reign of death which was its result.

The third difficulty concerns the *person*, the individual human being created in the image of God. If the essence of sin is wilful disobedience, then the person has not only turned away from God and lost his communion with him; he stands in a permanent relationship of rebellion against God. It is not possible for a man to be in a position of neutrality or to be as yet unformed in his potential relationship with God; that relationship already exists by virtue of his being a person in the image of God to begin with, and it can only be right or wrong. Justification is putting right this wrong relationship, something which can only be achieved by a submission of the person in faith to the person of Christ. Once that is accomplished, the sanctification of the nature must logically follow, since the person redeemed by grace is then empowered by the Holy Spirit of grace, who sets his will free from bondage and purifies his nature. The doctrine of deification, by seeking to make of nature something which it is not, obscures this and leads mankind into a false hope.

It will be seen from the above that the doctrine of justification depends on the most careful distinction between person and nature as radical concepts, and the precise relating of the will to each. It is a remarkable fact that when these things are misunderstood a distortion results, in which the idea of justification is compromised or even eliminated. Western theology has seen this happen in our own time as a result of the development of the idea of corporate personality (particularly with respect to the 'body of Christ') which effectively subordinates person to nature, thereby returning *sub alia specie* to a pre-Chalcedonian nature-Christology which has no room for either the penal substitutionary Atonement of Christ or for justification by faith in him.

A system of doctrine stands or falls as a whole, and statements at one level will usually be found both to depend on assumptions made at another level and to influence a wide range of themes whose interrelationship may not always be apparent from a simple logical analysis. In the case of justification by faith and Orthodox theology, the real difficulty lies at a deeper level, in the Orthodox view of original sin; and that in turn depends on an understanding of the will which, by missing the point that will expresses nature, fails to keep fully in line with the Christology of the Sixth Ecumenical Council in 681. Western theologians anxious to pursue the subject in discussions with the Orthodox must first of all penetrate to this level of understanding and reach agreement there. Unless this is done, the whole question of justification by faith will continue to appear irrelevant to Eastern theology, and as a result will risk being jettisoned altogether as of less than fundamental importance for Christian faith.

6

JUSTIFICATION AND ROMAN CATHOLICISM

George Carey

'There's no resisting an idea when its time has come', claimed David Steel when the Social Democratic Party began in 1980. Whatever view we might hold of the SDP it is a fact that an idea can launch an entirely new movement and also cause a radical conceptual break with all that preceded it. Such was the impact of the doctrine of justification by faith in the sixteenth century. It claimed that the heart of the Gospel is the *'Justificatio impii'*, the justification of the ungodly, meaning their forgiveness and acceptance through Christ. The Augsburg Confession of 1530 declared that: 'We became righteous toward God by grace for Christ's sake and through faith.' (*'Homines gratis justificantur propter Christum per fidem.'*)

This central idea split the Church in two, divided Europe and brought the Protestant Churches into being. And to this day the Lutheran Church together with many other Protestant communities declare that justification by faith is the 'first and principal article' of the Christian faith, the 'leaven' which makes the dough rise and the issue on which the whole ecumenical problem stands or falls.[1] The first Assembly of the World Council of Churches (1948) noted concerning Catholic–Protestant relationships that the subject of justification constitutes 'our deepest difference'.

What, then, is the curious business all about? In this short chapter we shall outline the nature of the problem and then we shall proceed to analyse four aspects of the doctrine as it bears upon the ecumenical debate.

1 Transformation versus Declaration

The question 'How can I find peace of mind before a holy God?' was very much a concern of the medieval period. The Church at the time was in no doubt that an answer was at hand through the ministrations and ordinances of the Church. Grace was viewed as springing from God and flowing sacramentally through the life of the Church, anointing the faithful who sought grace through the proper channels. Medieval Christians developed an elaborate structure which distinguished between various types and grades of grace. While it was from the same giver that all grace originated, the purposes for which he gave it varied – hence the proliferation of terms, 'justifying', 'habitual', 'created', 'uncreated' grace, and so on. For example, justifying grace was held to be conferred at the moment of justification (baptism) and to remain thereafter as part of the permanent state of the soul, a spiritual 'habitus'. Grace is thus 'infused' into the believer's life, and by its co-operation with the renewed human being goodness and righteousness 'inherent' in us (*justitia inhaerens*) result. This theology of salvation as a continuous process starting with the sacrament of baptism and culminating in the last rites was no doubt encouraged by the general tendency of the Western Church since the time of Augustine to consider justification as a process by which we are made ethically righteous. Indeed, Augustine interpreted the verb *'justificare'* as 'to make righteous' – a ghastly error due partly to Augustine's ignorance of New Testament Greek. For him justification was an inclusive concept which 'includes both the *event* of Justification (brought about by operating grace) and the *process* of Justification (brought about by co-operating grace)'.[2] Justification was, therefore, believed to be a transforming process by which we are being made righteous and so transformed into the likeness and image of God.

Martin Luther's experience of finding the grace of God in Christ introduced him to a wholly new understanding of justification. That experience coupled with his discovery of the meaning of 'the righteousness of God' in Paul's letter to the Romans led him to enunciate the teaching that justification is not a divine *process* by which man is being progressively saved, but a divine *declaration* that as of now he is saved. We have no righteousness of our own with which to contribute to, or co-operate with, God's saving work. Christ's righteousness is 'imputed' to us and his atoning merit is the ground of our salvation.

The antithesis between the 'transformation' and 'declaration' viewpoints is central to the historical differences between the Catholic and Protestant traditions. Catholic criticism of the *sola fide* doctrine was principally directed at its apparent disregard for the real renewal of the individual. Justification on these terms seemed to be a simple acquittal, something external which leaves us as we are, unrighteous. Although the Ratisbon Conversations of 1541 led to considerable agreement between Catholic and Lutheran spokesmen concerning the nature of justification, the polemical atmosphere was too highly charged for these to have any significance. This unhappy state of affairs lasted until Hans Küng, a promising Catholic research student at Tübingen University contributed his PhD thesis to the discussion. His dissertation, *Justification: The Doctrine of Karl Barth and a Catholic Reflection*[3] endeavoured to show that no substantial areas of difference actually exist between Barth's understanding of justification by faith and that of the Tridentine canons. Küng's well-researched and thorough piece of original study has in the main been accepted by both Catholic and Protestant theologians, thus raising hopes that the area of our 'deepest difference' might become the centre for reconciliation and restoration.

2 'Really real' Agreement?

But quite recently the accepted notion that basic rapprochement has been reached on the doctrine of justification has been challenged by Alistair McGrath.[4] McGrath argues that the only thing Küng has shown Trent and Barth do have in common is an anti-Pelagian Christocentric theology of justification. Furthermore, McGrath argues, Küng's appeal to certain modern Catholic theologians who also agree with the forensic interpretation of justification is beside the point. This, after all, is only an appeal to theological 'opinion'. What really counts is the weight of the magisterium which has not in any way altered its teaching that justification is a matter of being made righteous.

Of course, McGrath has a point. The problem Protestant scholars constantly have in discussion with their Roman Catholic counterparts is the twofold form in which Catholic dogma is expressed. Representative Catholic theologians are often astonishingly amenable, co-operative and of one mind with their Protestant colleagues. Dialogue thus often appears to achieve much – only to be apparently negated by the more doctrinaire, colder and less co-operative attitude of the teaching office. Is McGrath correct, then, in stating that nothing has really changed? And is it the case that this doctrine still remains our most intractable problem?

We need not share McGrath's pessimism. Küng's attempt was not an honourable failure but a most discerning piece of theological scholarship, revealing substantial areas of agreement. Moreover Protestants and Catholics have over the last thirty years or so taken the trouble to listen to one another on this subject, which before thay hardly did. Polemics – which someone defined as 'the dialogue of the deaf' – has been replaced by ecumenical exchanges aimed at exploring the areas of agreement and disagreement between us. This approach has uncovered layers of deep misunderstanding which is part of the discovery of how much we really have in common. As we saw earlier, the sorest point in Catholic objections to the Protestant interpretation was that its 'forensic' doctrine, by which the sinner is declared righteous through Christ, appeared to treat the actual removal of sin with dangerous indifference. A declaration that someone is acquitted seems to suggest that he is really still the same old sinner – a 'legal fiction', then, was the Catholic condemnation of the Protestant view.

Sola fide appeared to neglect the ethical aspect of the Gospel – love and good works. Such a doctrine seemed to lead straight to individualism and anti-nomianism. The Reformers constantly tried to show that this criticism was groundless but the bitterness was so deep that convergence of thought was not possible. In point of fact no Protestant theologian will affirm a 'purely' forensic concept of justification as if it is merely and exclusively an external matter. The doctrine simply states that when God declares a man just, so he is – not in himself, however, but in Christ. The other side of the coin, however, is that he is now a new creation indwelt by the Holy Spirit; a child of God in whom the work of grace has begun. The understanding of justification as primarily a legal metaphor does not, therefore, exclude the fact of the individual's renewal. Both Trent and the Reformers were one in understanding that God's grace is effective for personal change.

If the basic misunderstanding as to whether justification excludes renewal of the individual has now been cleared up, progress has also been made concerning the meaning of the word itself. There is now widespread recognition by many Catholic theologians that an accurate definition of justification demands a forensic context. Herding Meyer, for example, sums up the present state of scholarship on the subject as follows:

> The Reformation doctrine of justification has for some time had an importance and increasing number of Catholic advocates. Catholic theologians seem nowadays to have relieved their Protestant colleagues from the work of having to justify the doctrine of justification and to defend it against the polemical deformations and condemnations to which it has been hitherto a victim.[5]

H. Volk, for example, examining justification states that 'the idea of imputation and thus the forensic dimension cannot be dropped'.[6] M. Schmaus commends the teaching of the Reformers thus: 'The Reformers teach that God truly pardons sin. If then God declares the sinner justified he is made wholly just. According to the Reformers, God doesn't just pretend to act as if the person were not a sinner.'[7]

Therefore, far from Küng being an unrepresentative Catholic whose enthusiasm for ecumenism led him into making sweeping unsubstantiated claims, it is clear that his pioneering work has truly enabled theologians to see extensive agreement between the two estranged sides. McGrath's mistake, I submit, is to ignore the considerable Catholic weight of opinion which now supports the forensic interpretation. While it is true that the magisterium has not actually made any statements that indicate a change of heart in the Vatican, we must observe that it has also not uttered any statement which has condemned this shift in interpretation. Modern Catholicism in any case no longer proceeds by conscientiously toeing the party line, and in an increasing number of instances the line taken by the holy office is cheerfully ignored by many if not most Roman Catholic scholars.

3   The Place of Good Works

Among the most significant agreements between Catholics and Protestants is that salvation is all of grace. Summarising the doctrinal decisions of Trent, Küng declares: 'The justification of all through redemption in Christ by God's verdict is exclusively God's work: this is Catholic teaching.'[8] The great majority of Catholic theologians emphasise the primacy of God's grace which excludes human merit and boasting. Rahner points out that every human activity is linked to the gratuitous and unmerited grace of God.[9]

And yet if anything still keeps Catholics and Protestants apart, it is the idea that our own good works have some value in the scheme of salvation. Protestants remain suspicious of

Catholic insistence upon the centrality of grace because it has
seemed to them that the concept of 'inherent' grace implies
that our standing before God is somehow influenced by the
moral and spiritual initiatives we take. In my essay on this
subject in *The Great Acquittal*,[10] I drew attention to this
somewhat neglected aspect of justification and argued that
further clarification was needed on our attitude to the importance of human merit. It is good to report that steps have been
taken which show considerable convergence of thought.

First of all, Catholic theologians, who still prefer to use
Catholic terminology, acknowledge freely that even when we
talk of infused grace we are always referring to *God's* grace
given to men not to something which becomes our own
possession or resource. The Council of Trent, it is claimed, was
as anxious as the Reformers to preserve the Church from
Pelagianism. Fighting on two fronts it argued that *'justitia
inhaerens'* is indeed *'our* righteousness' (against the Reformers), but 'not *our own* righteousness' as if it stemmed from
ourselves (against Pelagianism). As we saw earlier, the background to this was discussion concerning the place of human
acts of goodness in the Christian life. The Reformers seemed to
make faith an 'external' thing, making no difference to the
heart of man and his behaviour. This was meaningless to many
Catholics who appealed to Augustine's statement (Paul's originally!) that 'faith works through love'.[11] Luther and his followers were therefore castigated as mischievous people who
ignored the ethical dimensions of faith.

Today, however, Catholic theologians defend Luther from
his critics.

> For Luther, faith is something alive and active ... faith
> cannot exist without love and without good works. Justify-
> ing faith is effective and of necessity related to love. The
> performing of works is so much part of justifying faith that
> we cannot speak of faith where these works are absent.[12]

But if clarity is thus reached concerning the importance of
good works to the Protestant Christian, Catholic theologians

are still anxious to establish that Catholic theology does not end up in a form of semi-Pelagianism. Catholic writers frequently appeal to the Council of Trent's statement that the '*causa efficiens*' of justification is 'the merciful God who freely washes and sanctifies us'.[13] Later in a statement against the Reformers' emphasis on faith, the Council says defensively:

> We may be said to be justified freely, in the sense that nothing that precedes justification, neither faith nor works, merits the grace of justification, for 'if out of grace, then not in virtue of works, otherwise (as the same Apostles say) grace is no longer grace'.[14]

As always, Rahner's contribution to this issue is original. He argues that it is a mistake to bring merit into opposition with grace. Every human act, he contends, is linked with grace which is absolutely gratuitous and unmerited and is only acceptable to God as an act of grace in us. The proper context for merit, according to Rahner, is not that of grace and salvation but of the Christian life.[15]

This leads into our second observation concerning developments in this area – that Catholic writers are themselves more critical these days of the concept of merit as being a meaningful theological idea.[16] The doctrine clearly led to abuse in medieval times and it is still possible that in some Church circles today – within Protestant as well as Catholic Churches – Christians will be found who believe that what we do has some bearing upon our future salvation, either as something additional to the merits of the Son of God, or, more likely, as good deeds which will somehow be taken into account on the day of judgment. Modern Catholicism is vocal in agreeing with historic Protestantism that this is a disastrous mistake.

Catholic theologians are as anxious these days as Protestants always have been to stress that 'merit' should not be understood as our attempt to stockpile heavenly credit. Rather, they insist, we should note that it refers to that dynamic quality of human existence in which God's grace meets with our response issuing in love and obedience. Trent itself declared: 'A Christian should have no inclination either to rely on himself or to glory in himself instead of the Lord whose goodness towards all men is such that *he wants his gifts to be* their merits.'[17] This last phrase is taken from Augustine who subordinated everything in the Christian life to divine grace.[18] Yet Augustine was quick to respond that the supremacy of grace within human freedom did not crush our free self-offering. Modern Catholic thinkers have developed the theological tension between grace and freedom and it is in this context that they wish to discuss the doctrine of merit. It is not a thing by which we purchase salvation, it is 'simply the reality of men . . . it is the fruit of the whole man acting under God's motion'.[19]

If all are agreed that Christ's death is the meritorious cause of salvation and his grace is at the heart of all human response, we are entitled to ask is 'merit', therefore, a helpful expression to use at all of our response to the Gospel? The short answer must be 'no' – the term is misleading and will always remain a centre of misunderstanding and controversy. Catholic theologians embracing it will always be forced to justify what they mean by it in the light of the statements they make about grace, and Protestant theologians in rejecting the term will then have to explain what they affirm positively about the place of human activity in the Christian life. But language which obliges you to keep explaining what you do not mean by it is burdensome rather than useful. The Catholic theologian O. Pesch argues vigorously that we must adopt a new terminology to express more precisely what we mean:

> The doctrine of merit is not a fundamental connection of faith which may never be given up, but a theological affirmation which can be allowed to drop or which can be replaced by better theological statements and analogies, without weakening the message of salvation in the process.[20]

I suggested in *The Great Acquittal* that the New Testament concept of 'reward' is a promising replacement term because it is a neutral word historically, untainted by contact with any particular form of interpretation which might make it un-acceptable to me or another. Both traditions therefore can come straight at it, seeking an analysis of the concept of works in the light of New Testament teaching. Indeed, this idea of 'reward' as used repeatedly by the Lord Jesus himself carries a strong reminder that morality is intrinsic to faith, never extrin-sic. The man who buries his talents, who remains in a state of moral inertia, is condemned by Christ, while the reward for faithful activity is pictured as wider scope for more activity of the same kind (Matt. 25:21, 23). Doing cannot be divorced from being: 'By their works you shall know them.' Also, we must observe, a clear line of New Testament teaching shows that as well as good works being an indication of our nature as Christians, they have a definite eschatological reference. While they are not, indeed, the basis upon which eternal life is secured – Christ is the reference point for that – the obedient response of our lives in holy living and committed discipleship will be taken into account by the Lord. As the Augsburg Confession puts it: 'Upon them [good works] depends the difference between the saints in glory.'

Of course, it remains to be seen whether a theological term of such power as 'merit', which has become part of the Catholic Church's history and spiritual inheritance, can be replaced by a less pejorative word like 'reward'. It will depend, to a great extent, upon the willingness of theologians to allow New Testament categories to challenge inherited assumptions and to provide new categories for our thinking about the character of a believer in Christ. As I see it, it is only by our joint willingness to do our theological investigations in this context that we shall fully appreciate what the Gospel says about the relationship of faith and works.

However, it might be worth observing that the widespread agreement that grace is at the heart of all human goodness opens the possibility of distinguishing the act of justification from the process of living the Christian life, which the Refor-mers called sanctification. Whereas these two elements have thus far been made one in the Catholic interpretation of 'being made righteous', they are separated in Protestant theology which views them as two aspects of the one event of salvation. A separation of the two would not only be more accurate biblically but, I submit, would also convey what both sides are trying to preserve, namely that justification is a declaration of God's forgiveness in Christ with Christ's righteousness imputed to us – and that new life is given through the Spirit in the community of Christ. Just as justifying grace can never be without good works, so good works are never outside the operation of grace. This is a most important and significant agreement between Catholics and Protestants.

4   Justification by Faith and the Character of the Church

If justification by faith is our deepest difference it is astonishing that in R. P. O'Brien's two volumes on *Catholicism*, consisting of 1,186 printed pages, the expression occurs less than ten times, whereas 400 pages are given to a thorough examination of the Church. Does this suggest that justification by faith is merely a Protestant, or more precisely a Lutheran and evangelical obsession, which is after all of minor significance for the whole sweep of ecumenism? So it might appear until it dawns on us what Luther meant when he described it as the 'leaven' which makes the dough rise. He saw the wider implications of justification; according to him Christianity itself stands or falls on this single article. It affects or colours our understanding and interpretation of practically every other doctrine. And nowhere is it more relevant than with respect to the doctrine of the Church, and I believe that our new-found agreement on the meaning of justification should be extended from its primary basis in the lives of the believers into the corporate life of the Church.

It is a fact that from a Protestant perspective the Catholic doctrine of the Church is the most difficult ecumenical problem. At the centre of the problem is the notion that the Church is infallible or inerrant. This idea creates a conceptual impasse which is impossible to bridge. It is a little like an estranged couple wishing to return to their former happy relationship in a situation where one of them says: 'Darling, of course I love you and I long for us to be together again. Yes, we have so much in common and it is tragic to be apart. But in order to put the record straight about the past I want to say this – *I have not done anything wrong!*' Any chance of reconciliation on that basis is slim. But I don't wish to suggest that Catholic theologians are as outrageous as that – indeed, they are extremely sensitive to the difficulties which their understanding of the Church creates for other Christians. It is true, however, that the doctrine of the indefectibility of the Church poses a real problem and will remain so until the doctrine of justification is allowed to play its part in defining the nature of the Church and the nature of sacramentality.

But what precisely does this mean? Two aspects of the doctrine bear upon the character of the Church.

(a) 'Simul justus et peccator' and an indefectible Church
At one time it was believed that the Reformation concept of the sinner as being at one and the same time 'righteous and yet a sinner' was incompatible with the Roman Catholic system. Catholic distaste focused on what was considered to be a mistaken view of Christian human nature – that a Christian was still imprisoned by his sin and in some sense unregenerate. Even Karl Rahner misunderstood this:

> The Catholic doctrine of justification will always emphasize that we become and are God's children through God's grace, and that in justification the Holy Spirit is given to us ... This reality is not merely an ideological fiction, not merely 'as if' but the true reality of man himself ... he ceases in a true sense to be a 'sinner'.[21]

The Reformation view then appeared to Catholic writers to be an ontological mistake, because if the Christian man was not truly made new, made alive in the Spirit, the Protestant formula was an inadequate expression of the Christian life.

And yet today there is widespread agreement that the formula is a correct analysis of the condition of the believer in

Christ. It is fully acceptable to Catholics in its existential and theological context, which is the state of human beings in the overlap of the two Adams. While we are redeemed and restored to God here and now by the second Adam we still experience moral and spiritual weakness and the power of sin in our lives. It is therefore recognised by modern theologians on both sides that the formula is not expressing a static view of humanity but revealing the twofold position of the Christian before a holy and loving God. 'In myself, apart from Christ, I am a sinner: In Christ, apart from myself, I am not a sinner.' Thus said Luther. This is not greatly different from Friest's observation: 'The Catholic Christian acknowledges these two states which are constantly expressed in the liturgy, "I am the chief of sinners", and "I thank you for having saved me".'[22]

But the formula can be extended beyond the individual into the life of the Church. When we fail to apply this insight to the corporate body of the Church we make it a rigid, static, 'sinless' institution which replaces Christ as the determinative reference point. Such was the Roman Catholic concept of the Church before Vatican II. The ecclesiology of the First Vatican Council and the contents of *Paster Aeternus* emphasised hierarchical dependence upon that once described in the Constitution as Romanus Pontifex. There is still a significant section of the Roman Church which believes that these categories correctly adumbrate Catholic doctrine. For them the faith of the Church is always kept free of error. The magisterium, that is the teaching office of the Church, is a certain guide for the faithful, and there can be no doubt that Christ's body under the faithful leadership of an infallible Pope will be preserved in the true faith. Unity according to this model consists in the non-Roman communities' returning home since by definition the Roman Church has not deviated from God's truth.

The ecclesiological teaching of Vatican II, however, introduced a more hopeful perspective by its understanding of the Church as a 'pilgrim' body journeying through history.[23] With the major emphasis laid upon the idea of communion with God and one another in the Christian body, a shift was made from the thought of a hierarchy dominated by one man to that of an ecclesial communion with gifts to share. Of course, the concept of hierarchy was still there but the idea of the episcopal college replaced the older understanding of all ministries subsisting in the papal office. This was a most important ecumenical step, for whereas the ecclesiology of Vatican I was the ecumenism of 'come home – all is forgiven', that of the second Council amounted to a recognition that other Churches separated from Rome were not necessarily separated from God. It is true that the Council asserted that in the Roman Church 'the Church of Christ subsists', but that statement does not mean that Christ's people are only to be found there. The ecumenical programme of Vatican II was, therefore, 'let us find unity together – and let us find it in one another'.

The notion of the Church as a 'pilgrim' body offers more scope for understanding the truth of *simul justus et peccator* as a description of her. This is, beyond doubt, a correct although sad diagnosis of her condition in time – a holy people, certainly, in Christ, yet rent asunder by sin, heresy and division. A recognition of the Church's peccability and actual sin carries with it the benefit of discovering that unity consists of finding our reconciliation not merely in one another but in Christ the Saviour who is the centre of our faith. As Moltmann wrote: 'The nearer we come to Christ, the nearer we come together.'[24] And in his light we are unworthy, and it becomes plain that no Church has kept the whole faith of Christ untarnished from human error, misunderstanding and wrong. So there can be no unity worthy of the name unless there is acknowledgment of the Church as sinful, both morally and intellectually, in its historical manifestation.

What then of the concept that the Church is 'indefectible'? This term has been used of late by Catholic theologians to avoid the embarrassment that would be caused by saying straight out that the Church can do no wrong. But if by this term we mean that the Church will be kept free from error in time, this is not only palpably untrue; it assumes also a false diagnosis of humanity in its individual and corporate aspects.

If the limbs are not error-free it is not meaningful to say that the body is. If, however, we understand the word as having an eschatological reference it is perfectly possible to see it as meaning that God's hand is upon his people leading them towards that full purity of his truth which is his will for his people. Seen in this way 'indefectibility' may have considerable significance and will surely tie in with Paul's image of the Church as a bride 'without spot or wrinkle'. It is quite evident that as far as this world goes there can be no complete realisation of the eschatological notion of indefectibility in a divided Christendom. *Schism* is a deformation of God's high ideals for his people and is in itself sufficient reason why all who call themselves Christians should strive for that unity which is his will.

(b) *'Justification by Faith' and God's Salvation*　A thorny issue between Catholics and Protestants is the way in which the doctrine of justification affects our understanding of the ministry and sacraments of the Church. Evangelicals have no desire to impose a 'low Church' view of ministry on those who prefer an ornate style of celebration, neither is it their intention to replace an emphasis upon a 'real presence' in the sacrament of Holy Communion by a 'real absence'. In fact, there are many evangelical Christians who hold a high view of the sacraments and their place in the Church. The point at issue – and it is nothing to do with ceremony (whether we like our spiritual fare plain and simple, or highly seasoned and rich) – is that the sacraments of the Church must declare the same doctrine that we preach and teach. If the doctrine of justification says to the heart of the believer, 'You are ransomed, healed, restored, forgiven', the sacraments must not then say 'You must strive to be accepted and you must come back here often to be atoned for'. The sacrament of Holy Communion, the Eucharist, the Mass – the term we use is of no great significance – is also the sacrament of our justification. It sets forth the basis upon which we are forgiven and declares to our hearts that Christ's perfect sacrifice has dealt with our sins decisively. The Anglican–Roman Catholic International document on the Eucharist shows agreement between the representative theologians on the fact that Christ's death was an unrepeatable sacrifice for sin. So we need to explore differences which go beyond that, and seem to obscure it. What meaning, for instance, can we give to the Mass as an 'unbloody sacrifice', and to the priest standing *in persona Christi*, when the sacrament declares that the way to God is now open through the 'once-for-all' offering of the great High Priest?

The same 'knock-on' principle holds for other ministries and sacraments in the Church. While it is proper to speak of them as 'effective' signs, in the sense that in and by them God's grace is made available to all who trust in him, the idea of automatic grace – *gratia ex opere operato* – is not consistent with 'justification by faith', which implies that we have to respond personally to God's free offer of life. And the doctrine of justification affects the character of Christian ministry also. Scripture and the testimony of Christian history encourage us to have a high doctrine of ministry in its major sense of serving God and his people. But the doctrine of justification stresses that mediatorship and priesthood belong to Christ essentially and never in any real sense to us. All we can do in our ministry is point to his perfect ministry and priesthood and rejoice in the benefits which flow from them. Of course important ecumenical issues flow from this; if, for instance, we bring the doctrine of justification into line with other teachings, have terms like 'sacrifice' and 'priesthood' any value for us? On the other hand, acknowledging their part in Catholic tradition and spirituality, may they still be retained without being a major stumbling-block to unity?

Conclusion

We have been able to point to great areas of understanding between Catholics and Protestants on the doctrine of justification by faith and this is cause for great rejoicing. To find basic agreement here of all places is in itself a testimony to the more tolerant times we live in, as well as to the tenacity of theologians like Küng who have struggled to show that bridges can be built across the most hostile of terrain. If I may be so bold as to address my fellow evangelicals, I venture to say to them that as on this issue of the doctrine of justification by faith we should note the great desire of Catholic theologians to understand and learn from Protestants, so we too must endeavour to understand Catholic perspectives and enter into sympathetic dialogue. It's all too easy to hide behind precious shibboleths of our faith, signposts of our historical pilgrimage – but our journey is to Christ and with Christ. Surely if our ecumenical theology is done in his light and for his glory, we shall move away from the bitternesses of the past into the unity of the Spirit which is God's desire for his broken Church.

7

THE JUSTIFIED MINISTER AT WORK

David Wheaton

(This chapter was originally one of the Charles Simeon Lectures at Trinity Episcopal School for Ministry, Ambridge, Pennsylvania, USA, given in October 1983.)

In *The Pilgrim's Progress* John Bunyan tells how his hero, Christian, is taken while in the Interpreter's House to see a portrait of

> a very grave person . . . with eyes lifted up to heaven; the Best of Books in his hand; the law of truth written upon his lips; the world was behind his back; it stood as if it pleaded with men; and a crown of gold did hang over his head.
>
> 'I have showed thee this picture first,' said the Interpreter, 'because the man whose picture this is, is the only man whom the Lord whither thou art going hath authorised to be thy guide . . .'

The Christian minister has the tremendous privilege of being the guide of souls on their pilgrimage to heaven.

Paul was deeply aware of this when he told his friends in Corinth that 'if the ministry of condemnation had glory, the ministry of righteousness exceeds much more in glory', since its ministers are heralds of the new covenant, a covenant of the Spirit, who brings life.[1] Bishop Michael Baughen has on occasion said that to be a stipendiary Christian minister is like the joy of Moses' mother – who by God's providence was paid to do the one thing which above all else she wanted to do.

The greatest service any Christian can do for fellow human beings is to lead them to faith in Jesus Christ. This is a task which Christ has committed to his whole church. It was the final dominical commission (Acts 1:8 – where the command 'you shall be my witnesses' is prefaced by the promise of the Spirit 'you shall receive power'), and it was duly taken to heart by the members of the early Church.[2]

To pass on the understanding of what it means to be justified by faith was and is a charge to every Christian, and this is the way in which Protestant Christians have understood the power of the keys committed to Simon Peter. This power, which Jesus gave him at Caesarea Philippi (Matt. 16:19), was extended to a wider circle of disciples in the upper room on the first Easter evening (John 20:25 – the context nowhere suggests that this appearance was restricted to the eleven); then on the day of Pentecost Peter showed how it is to be exercised by proclaiming the terms on which God welcomes sinful human beings into his kingdom.[3]

The Task of the Church

When Paul reminds the Ephesian Christians of the gifts bestowed on God's people through the coming of the Holy Spirit, he says that they were given 'to equip the saints for the work of ministry' (Eph. 4:12). The word used here for ministry (*diakonia*) is reminiscent of Jesus' own words to his disciples at the Last Supper when he drew attention to his own vision for and style of leadership – 'I am among you as one who serves' (Luke 22:27, where the verb used of serving has the same root).

Much has been written in recent years about the servant role of the Church, and the Lausanne Covenant has sought to provide for evangelicals a clear statement of the importance of both evangelism and social action in the Church's service to the world. On the local front, the parish church is called to be the servant church in the life of the community, and in many places today buildings and plant are being reordered to take this responsibility into account. A redevelopment in Bristol during the 1970s with which one of Oak Hill's former students was involved, whereby three former parish churches became the 'Easton Family Centre', is an indication of the direction in which churches are moving today.

During an interregnum the young people of a West End church in London's bed-sitter-land organised a questionnaire to discover what were the pressing needs of the parish area to which the new incumbent should address himself. It came as no surprise that loneliness came out as the greatest need: what was surprising was the extent to which this was experienced by men and women of all ages.

In consequence that church redeveloped part of its plant to improve catering and toilet facilities so that the needs of the community could be met by accommodating a playgroup, old people's lunch club, coffee bar for young people (and the not-so-young), and other local requirements. Such use meant that the church once again moved towards the centre of the community: no longer was the building frequented only by the faithful at times of divine service, but people were coming and going at all hours through the week. Non-churchgoers were frequently on the premises and became familiar with the clergy as they went about their daily business.

Most congregations operate as a series of concentric circles with the minister at the centre, surrounded by a group of highly committed men and women, and radiating out via folk with lesser degrees of commitment to those with minimal contact on the fringe of Church life. Evangelism in many cases consists of leading those from the fringe closer to the centre of Church life, and therefore it is important for healthy growth that a church should be constantly replenishing its fringe.

In order to do this work effectively, a clear grasp of justification by faith is necessary so that we know what needs to be set before our contemporaries as we approach them with the Gospel. Evangelism often presents God as a 'God of the gaps' – one who can meet our felt needs (loneliness, fear, worry, aimlessness). This by itself can leave the impression that the Gospel is only for the inadequate. All evangelism must be related to what is ever human being's basic need, whether felt or not – need, that is, for forgiveness and a right relationship with God – and to everyone's basic problem – that innate self-centredness which has led to rebellion against God and which the Bible calls sin.

This point needs to be stressed because sometimes those who make a profession of faith in Jesus Christ lay the emphasis on what they are doing for God, as if by inviting Christ into their lives they are conferring a favour on him, rather than acknowledging what he has done for them at their point of deepest need. It was while we were yet sinners that Christ died for us (Rom. 5:8), and the apostle John defines love unequivocally in his first Epistle – 'In this is love, not that we loved God but that he loved us and sent his Son to be the expiation for our sins' (1 John 4:10).

This was the emphasis in the evangelistic preaching of the early Church, as the following texts show:

Let it be known to you therefore, brethren, that through this man [Christ] forgiveness of sins is proclaimed to you, and by him every one that believes is freed from everything from which you could not be freed by the law of Moses (Acts 13:38–9, Paul in the synagogue at Antioch).

The times of ignorance God overlooked, but now he commands all men everywhere to repent, because he has fixed a day on which he will judge the world in righteousness by a man whom he has appointed . . . (Acts 17:30–1, Paul on Mars Hill).

Repent and be baptised every one of you in the name of Jesus Christ for the forgiveness of your sins (Acts 2:38, Peter in Jerusalem on the day of Pentecost).

I did not shrink from declaring to you . . . and teaching you . . . testifying both to Jews and to Greeks of repentance to God and of faith in our Lord Jesus Christ (Acts 20:20–1, Paul to the Ephesian elders at Miletus).

Felix came with his wife Drusilla, who was a Jewess; and he sent for Paul and heard him speak upon faith in Christ Jesus. And as he argued about justice and self-control and future judgment, Felix was alarmed . . . (Acts 24:24–5, Paul at

Caesarea before the Roman governor Felix).

... I send you to open their eyes, that they may turn from darkness to light and from the power of Satan to God that they may receive the forgiveness of sins ... Wherefore, O King Agrippa, I ... declared ... that they should repent and turn to God ... (Acts 26:18–23, Paul's testimony to King Herod Agrippa at Caesarea; the whole passage deserves careful study as a résumé by the apostle of his ministry).

In this wide variety of situations, to the intelligentsia, the nobility, immigrants and ordinary people of their day, Jews and Gentiles alike, the apostles proclaimed the same message. We in our turn must not be ashamed of that Gospel, for evangelism, as has been said, is one beggar telling another beggar where to find bread. Some years ago when he was Archbishop of York, Donald Coggan wrote in his *Diocesan News* about the decline in the numbers of ordinands and had this to say:

We have presented a God too small for this space age; a God who would seem to be a sort of over-sized ecclesiastic, interested in little else than ecclesiastical matters. We have all too often failed to present a Christ magnificent in the greatness of his love and power, vast in the scope of his redemption. No wonder there is uncertainty of belief, a failure to commit oneself for life.

That fact can also explain why there are so few truly committed lay people in our churches. A further glance at the contexts of the passages of preaching, exhortation and testimony quoted above, and at other such passages in the New Testament, will show that Jesus and his followers did not soft-pedal the challenge of the Gospel, nor were they in any doubt as to man's universal need of this good news.

Objections are sometimes made that people cannot understand the language and pictures the Bible uses when referring to sin and forgiveness. They may not, but the cure for that is that folk should learn what these things mean as they are explained and taught by those of us whose responsibility this is. Plenty of people will spend time and money in learning the language and technicalities of photography or car-maintenance in order to enjoy the fruits of such a hobby, and there is no reason why they should not be encouraged to view the message of the Bible in a similar light.

If we ourselves know what it is to be justified by faith, we must make the sharing of that knowledge in evangelising others a top priority. Rightly did the Anglican Congress in Toronto in 1963 declare that 'the church that lives to itself will die by itself'. The same is true of the individual Christian.

The Task of the Ordained Minister

If the work of the whole local church is to minister to the local community, what is the role of the 'ministry' (those set apart officially by ordination or licensing or other form of commissioning within the fellowship)? Ephesians 4:12 again tells us. The various persons with God-given spiritual gifts of evangelism and pastoral care are themselves gifts to God's church, given 'to equip the saints for the work of ministry' (RSV's comma in the translation is misleading). We must consider how the pastor can best discharge this responsibility of equipping Christians to serve.

The New Testament uses three main pictures (among several others) to point to the three main fields of the church's action in which a pastor has this responsibility. We may tabulate them as follows:

A temple – a place for worship — speaks of the Christian's obligations towards God (1 Cor. 3:16; Eph. 2:19–22; 1 Pet. 2:4–6 etc.).

A body – an instrument for service — speaks of the Christian's obligations towards the wider

community (1
Cor. 12:12–27;
Eph. 4:4, 15–
16).

A family – a unit for fellowship and growth – speaks of the
Christian's obli-
gations towards
one another
(Eph. 2:19–22;
Gal. 4:4–7;
Rom. 8:14–17;
1 Pet. 2:17; and
the use of
'brother' in 1
John).

These pictures, however, only assume their fullest meaning in
our minds when we know they are relevant *for us*: when, in
other words, we know ourselves to be Christians, those who
have been saved to serve and enriched to give in this threefold
way. The need all Christians have of this knowledge brings us
to the crux of the matter, the most important pastoral consequence of justification by faith. This is the doctrine of
assurance, which is the key to all the work of the reformed
pastor. As, without water, indoor plants droop and shrivel, so
without assurance, worship, service and fellowship will wither
and flag.

If justification is only complete (as has traditionally been
argued in the pre-Reformation Western Church and post-
Reformation Roman church) when I have sufficiently co-
operated with the grace of God at work in me to develop in
myself the righteousness of Christ, I can never in this life be
sure of my standing with God. But that is not the religion of the
Bible: it can only lead, as Professor Richard Hanson points out
in a monograph quoted below, to making your religion an
anxious nagging at God, which New Testament Christianity
most emphatically is not.

But '. . . it is perfectly unnecessary to nag, because God has,
independently of your anxiety, gratuitously, unexpectedly and

inexplicably, given you everything in the way of salvation that you could possibly want in Christ. Luther recaptured by this process of thought the original joy and assurance and total absence of anxiety of the primitive Church.'[4] This is one great fruit of the doctrine of justification by faith.

The Christian pastor must therefore encourage a right understanding of assurance, and a true experience of it, by placing proper emphasis on what God has done in Christ. He must not lay his emphasis on what the believer has done in 'making a commitment', for that would be to revert to a doctrine of works!

A veteran evangelist of a previous generation frequently used to point those he led to Christ to John 6:37. Here the glorious promise that 'him who comes to me I will not cast out' is prefaced by the complementary statement that those who do come in faith to the Son are those whom the Father is giving to the Son. Our coming to the Son is our response to the Father's electing grace. A theologian on being asked when he was saved once replied: 'I have been saved three times. I was saved in eternity in the plan of God the Father, at Calvary through the atoning work of God the Son, and on –day, 19— by the converting work of God the Spirit.'

It is God's intention that Christians should enjoy their birthright of assurance. Hence the New Testament makes such clear statements as those in John 1:12; 5:24; 1 John 5:12, 13; and Rom. 8:14–17, 32–9. In his *Life of Dr R. W. Dale,*[5] A. W. Dale makes a sad comment about E. B. Pusey:

> The absence of joy in his religious life was only the inevitable effect of his conception of God's method of saving man; in parting with the Lutheran truth concerning justification he parted with the springs of gladness.

Similarly, James Denney writes:[6]

> Nothing is more characteristic of churches than their attitude to assurance, and the place they give it in their preaching and in their systems of doctrine. Speaking broadly, we may say

that in the Romish church it is regarded as essentially akin to presumption; in the Protestant churches it is a privilege or a duty, but in the New Testament religion it is simply a fact. This explains the joy which, side by side with the sense of infinite obligation, is the characteristic note of Apostolic Christianity.

In recent years the working of the Holy Spirit in renewal has brought this assurance into the lives of many Christians of all denominations, and so the lines are not today so clear-cut as Denney's statement suggests. However, what he says is still true of the doctrinal position officially represented by the Churches.

When, therefore, the Christian minister has the joy of leading others to an experience of justification by faith, it is important to follow up this step by introducing them to a programme of Bible study which will deepen their understanding of their new-found relationship with God in Christ by the Spirit. A chapter like Ephesians 1, for instance, will help them to discover all that God has done and is waiting to do for them in Christ.

The new Christian also can and should be introduced to the pictures mentioned above and made aware of the consequences.

'I am a stone in the temple, indwelt by the Holy Spirit and thus set apart for him' (see Eph. 2:19–22; 1 Cor. 6:19–20; 1 Pet. 2:4). In these days when Christian standards of personal morality are not so widely known or practised, it will be important to help the new Christian to work out the implications of the set-apart relationship.

'I am a member of the body, united to Christ the head, and so I have a special part to play for him' (see 1 Cor. 12:14–27). The wise pastor will look for and foster the gifts the new Christian can bring to the fellowship, and also use in reaching out for his Lord. The secret of a rural incumbent who was unusually successful in retaining his young candidates after their confirmation was contained in seven words, 'I always give them something to do.' Bishop Leslie Brown (formerly of

Namirembe and then St Edmundsbury and Ipswich) said some years ago,

> The real work of the Church is wherever men and women live and work – this is where the Church brings God to people. The people who can fulfil this work are those in close daily touch with men and women where they work and live. That is to say, the effective agents of the Church in their primary task are lay people. The job of the ordained servants of the Church is to equip themselves in every way possible to equip the lay people to fulfil directly their call. This is the primary task of the ordained ministry. They therefore give themselves to the pastoral care and counselling of the laity and they build them up in faith through word and sacrament. This is how I see it. The laity are not there to back up the clergy: the clergy are there to back up the laity.[7]

Much has been written elsewhere about the concept of 'every-member ministry', and new Christians must be introduced to this idea of their responsibility to be actively involved in the life of the Church. They must be shown that the more mundane tasks listed in Romans 12 are just as much spiritual gifts as the more spectacular ones of 1 Corinthians 12.

'I am a child in the family, adopted by God my heavenly Father, and therefore have full rights and privileges in the family' (see Gal. 4:4–7 and Rom. 8:14–17). As pastors we must encourage God's children to look to their Father for his loving provision and guidance as they serve him. Remembering that God is our heavenly Father, and we his heirs, will always bring confidence and joy. Furthermore, once we have helped people to discover the wonder of acceptance by the Father into his family, then we can underline for them the importance of fully accepting one another – see Romans 15:7. Thus family fellowship will grow.

One of the joys of belonging to a Christian congregation lies in the fact that it usually brings together men and women, old and young, from such a wide variety of backgrounds. In the house of God in these days people of many different social and cultural backgrounds are found together. Often, indeed, this is the only place where they are found together. At the distribution of Holy Communion it is very moving to notice the variety of hands held out to receive the elements – hands of different colour, stained with or trained for many different activities and occupations. The wise pastor (and the wise layman too!) will use his home to bring together individuals from the different groups and thus maximise both for himself and for his guests the joy of belonging to such an all-embracing family.

As relationships develop within the local church family there is one snare of which pastors must beware. This is the paradoxical temptation for them to feel the need to justify their position as leaders by endless frenzied activity. Many clergy feel it important to demonstrate their value to their congregations by the multiplicity of the things they *do* for their people. In our Anglican ordinal the emphasis is not only on what the minister does, but also on what he *is*. Professor Henri Nouwen brings this point out helpfully in his significant book on contemporary ministry, *The Wounded Healer*.[8] Time and again in pastoral ministry we are faced with the apostle's question, 'Who is sufficient for these things?' and time and again we must answer as he did, 'Our competence is from God, who has made us competent to be ministers of a new covenant . . .'[9] The Christian minister can rest in his knowledge of God's calling and his experience of God's enabling, and does not need to draw attention to what he is doing, as if he secretly hopes to be justified by works after all!

The Task of the Individual

Justification brings to the believer the imputed righteousness of Christ: and with that it gives a picture of what God intends to do in our lives. In undertaking henceforth to treat us as righteous for Jesus' sake, God also undertakes to transform us into Jesus' likeness. John Newton's testimony was:

> I am not what I ought to be,
> I am not what one day I hope to be,
> But, praise God, I am not what I used to be,
> And I am what I am by the grace of God.

When Jesus looked on Simon with all his weaknesses, he saw what he could make of him, 'So you are Simon . . .? You shall be called Cephas' (John 1:42). His vision for all his people is similar: we are all 'called to be saints' (Rom. 1:7; 1 Cor. 1:2; and see 1 Pet. 1:3–5).

Our task is, under the Holy Spirit's direction and with his enabling, to rebuild in our lives the image of Christ – that is, the holiness of character and lifestyle that was destroyed at the Fall and is destroyed afresh by our own individual waywardness and rebellion. Romans 5:1–5 shows that this is one of the consequences of being justified by faith. Classic Protestant theology has taught that justification is the work of a moment. God remits our sins and imputes to us the righteousness of Christ the moment we look to him in saving faith. Sanctification, however, which means growing into the likeness of Christ at every point of moral action, is the work of a lifetime. It too is achieved by faith, a daily looking to Jesus (see 2 Cor. 3:18), though not with a faith that opposes action, as when we stop working and cast ourselves on Christ instead for acceptance; rather, we look to Jesus now to energise action, the action of Christian good works. This process is again aided by our understanding of assurance: the fact that in Christ God has forgiven us assures us that we can now look him in the face, and confidently rely on him for help.

As a young soldier, the writer was encouraged to take a proper pride in his position, and to respond to increasing demands in the light of it, by the refrain constantly shrieked at him on the parade-ground: 'You're not in the army now – you're in the Brigade of Guards!' With this reminder, heads went up, chests were thrown out and everyone felt six inches taller. Similarly, the Christian may tell himself triumphantly: 'You're not an ordinary human being now – you're a child of God!'

Satan's ongoing activity is to accuse the brethren, and he often tries to cast doubts on our assurance. Indeed, Paul in Romans 8:31-7 may be reflecting in his questions some of the battles he himself had to fight as Satan sought to undermine his faith. Similarly Martin Luther, on an occasion when in a dream he had seen the full tale of his sins being listed in God's record book, is reputed to have told the recorder to list them all, adding many more, and then to write across the pages the reassuring promise of 1 John 1:7 – 'the blood of Jesus his Son cleanses us from all sin'.

One of the joys of knowing that we are accepted by God, not for our own efforts but through the righteousness of Christ, is that this then enables us to accept ourselves. Those who have gone even to the extreme of attempting suicide because of their feelings of failure or rejection can know the joy of a fresh start in life and in self-esteem because they are accepted in the beloved.[10]

We have no right to hate ourselves, and refuse ourselves forgiveness, and become self-destructive, when we know that God has loved and pardoned and saved us. The pastor's task then is to teach his flock the way of sanctification: how they are to grow up into that righteousness of Jesus which they have received as God's initial gift of the Christian life (see, for example, 2 Pet. 1:3–11). This is why Bible study and teaching must play an important part in the life of every church that is to be effective in carrying out its God-appointed tasks.

In teaching about sanctification pastors regularly take their congregations through the teaching of the Epistle to the Romans. Chapter 6 majors on setting out the implications of justification in the life of the baptised, and also contains two phrases which many have found to provide the secret of victorious Christian living. Verse 11 says 'consider yourselves . . .' and verse 13 says 'yield yourselves . . .' Here are acts of the mind and of the will, in response to Christ's death and resurrection, for us to know the reality of our incorporation into him. These commitments are at the heart of obedient and fruitful Christian discipleship.

While we emphasise the importance of accepting one

another as God in Christ has accepted us, we must beware of a selfish and insensitive way of imposing on the acceptance of our Christian friends. There have been those who take the line that 'since God has accepted me as I am, I will continue to be selfish, thoughtless, unloving, unreliable, or whatever it may be, and you must just go on accepting me.' This is obviously not a Christian attitude, and needs to be exposed as such. Any true experience of justification by faith will lead to a desire to develop in our lives our counterpart of the righteousness of Christ that God has imputed to us.

In this process an important element will be the regular examination of one's spiritual progress. In the context of coming to the Lord's table the apostle suggests that we should examine ourselves, and one of Cranmer's exhortations, that has been in Anglican usage since the Prayer Book of 1549, has stressed the value of this practice.[11] Traditionally, this was the purpose of the reading of the Ten Commandments (or at least our Lord's summary of the Law) at the start of the Communion service: modern liturgies (e.g. that of the Anglican Church of Chile) suggest alternative passages that can be used for this purpose, such as Matthew 5:3–12 (the beatitudes), 1 Corinthians 13:1–7 (the more excellent way), Galatians 5:16–24 (the fruit of the Spirit). The interest shown by Christians of many traditions in Richard Foster's recent *Celebration of Discipline*[12] reflects a desire on the part of many Christians to review and further their progress in the spiritual life.

In this connection there is a very real place for the Christian pastor to fill as a spiritual director to his flock. This does not necessarily entail the use of the confessional, and it is interesting that using the modern Roman rite of penance many Roman Catholic priests (especially those involved in spiritual renewal) have replaced the private confessional with services of corporate repentance.[13]

Once a pastor has made it known that he is available for private consultation (and an increasing number of clergy publish weekly times when they will be holding 'surgery' hours) he will find that numbers of people from outside as well as within the congregation value the opportunity to seek his advice and guidance. Some will come as genuine 'penitents', asking for the assurance of God's forgiveness of some action about which they have a deep sense of guilt. It was for such that our Reformers left open the door for private confession and absolution.[14]

When the pastor undertakes this ministry he should see it as a crutch for the spiritually lame, and not as a habit that fitter souls should be encouraged to form. The Prayer Book suggests that ideally the Christian will learn to deal with the guilt of specific sins privately in his or her deepening relationship with God. Where a formal confession and absolution are necessary, the exhortation in the Prayer Book (quoted in n. 14) makes it plain that the assurance of forgiveness should be based on the authority of God's Word rather than of God's minister. This has been at the heart of recent controversy over the proposed Church of England services for the reconciliation of a penitent, and many feel that the kind of absolution offered as an alternative in the Series Two (revised) revision of Morning and Evening Prayer could best provide both a solution to the theological problem and the required pastoral comfort. The wording used there is 'Christ Jesus came into the world to save sinners. Hear then the word of grace and the assurance of pardon: Your sins are forgiven for his sake.'[15]

In the long term the pastor will seek to help each Christian to know the Lord Jesus Christ more deeply as the great High Priest to whom we can come and on whom we can lean for pardon for past sin and strength to face future temptation. This is what the writer of the Letter to the Hebrews has in mind as he exhorts:

Since then we have a great high priest who has passed through the heavens, Jesus the Son of God, let us hold fast our confession. For we have not a high priest who is unable to sympathise with our weaknesses, but one who in every respect has been tempted as we are, yet without sin. Let us then with confidence draw near to the throne of grace, that we may receive mercy and find grace to help in time of need (4:14-16).

'In the above passage the word for 'confidence' has the root idea of 'telling everything'. God is the one who knows all about us, we know him as the one to whom all hearts are open, all desires known, and from whom no secrets are hidden, and so we can tell him all with no shocks or surprises. He knows all about us and accepts us as we are, restoring us when we are penitent, and so it is to him that we teach people to come for pardon. John Owen, the great Puritan writer, has said, 'there is no office of Christ that Satan labours so hard to obscure and overthrow as His priestly one'.[16] It is important then, whether we see ourselves in the Protestant role as the pastor, or the Catholic role as the priest, that we do nothing which would prevent Christians from developing their own relationship with Jesus Christ and learning to go to him for cleansing and strength.

This, surely, is the great goal of all our pastoral ministry, and brings us back to the note on which we began this chapter. The whole work of the justified minister is to bring people to Jesus Christ, who is 'made our wisdom, our righteousness and sanctification and redemption' (1 Cor. 1:30). The pastoral office consists of helping others to establish and strengthen their personal relationship with Christ, even as we ministers ourselves seek daily to strengthen our own, so that pastor and flock together may say with Charles Wesley:

> No condemnation now I dread,
> Jesus and all in Him is mine,
> Alive in Him, my living Head,
> And clothed in righteousness divine,
> Bold I approach the eternal throne
> And claim the crown, through Christ, my own.

That is the heart of Christian assurance; and to lead folk to the rich pastures of assurance, and to walk with them there until the day when they are taken to receive that promised crown of life, is the goal and the glory of all true pastoral care.

'Who is sufficient for these things? . . . our competence is from God, who has made us competent to be ministers of a new covenant' (2 Cor. 2:16; 3:5). And the first qualification for such ministry is to know oneself, sinner that one is, to be justified, here and now, by grace through faith.

8

LITURGY FOR THE JUSTIFIED

David Wheaton

(This chapter was originally one of the Charles Simeon Lectures at Trinity Episcopal School for Ministry, Ambridge, Pennsylvania, USA, given in October 1983.)

What we do and say in our worship will be determined by what we believe about the God who is the object of that worship. So too will the setting we provide for that worship. The vast cathedral with its soaring vaulted ceilings, the distant sounding ethereal notes of the choir and the gentle gradations from nave to chancel, presbytery and sanctuary with steps up at every stage, all speak of the majesty and greatness of the God who is transcendent. His nearness and immanence in his creation and among his people are more likely to be sensed in the modern church at the heart of the housing estate, planned to house God's people round his table as they join together to worship him in the language of everyday life. Both these aspects of God's being must be held in tension, and one of the concerns of twentieth-century liturgists must be to enable God's people to experience both in their worship.

'We are accounted righteous before God, only for the merit of our Lord and Saviour Jesus Christ by Faith, and not for our own works or deservings: wherefore, that we are justified by Faith only is a most wholesome Doctrine, and very full of comfort, as more largely is expressed in the Homily of Justification.' So runs the eleventh of the Thirty-Nine Articles of the Church of England. Because the Reformers had recently rediscovered the wholesome comfort of that doctrine, it had been their concern to make sure that it was proclaimed in their liturgies. Thus Gregory Dix comments on Cranmer's 1552 communion service, 'As a piece of liturgical craftsmanship it is in the first rank – once its intention is understood. It is *not* a disordered attempt at a catholic rite, but the only effective attempt ever made to give liturgical expression to the doctrine of "justification by faith alone".'[1]

It is our purpose in this essay to consider the place of this doctrine in Christian worship (and especially in the Lord's Supper, Eucharist or Holy Communion), looking at the way in which the Reformers of the sixteenth and revisers of the twentieth centuries have given it expression, and to make suggestions for those who will be involved in further revision, especially as the Church of England prepares to review her Alternative Service Book in 1990.

What do we do in Worship?

'The chief end of man is to glorify God and enjoy Him for ever.'[2] Down the ages man has sought to glorify God by recalling his mighty acts, reflecting in consequence on the character those acts have revealed, and praising him for both. This is seen time and again in the Psalms of the Old Testament,[3] and is highlighted in the glimpse we are given of the worship of heaven in the Book of Revelation. Here chapter 4 shows us representatives of the whole creation gathered in worship before their Creator and uniting in the refrain –

Worthy art thou, our Lord and God,
to receive glory and honour and power,
for thou didst create all things,
and by thy will they existed and were created.[4]

The following chapter shows the same representatives of God's creation together with the redeemed community joining in a song of praise to the Redeemer –

Worthy art thou to take the scroll and to open its seals,
for thou wast slain and by thy blood didst ransom men for
  God
from every tribe and tongue and people and nation,
and hast made them a kingdom and priests to our God,
and they shall reign on earth.

This refrain is then picked up by the wider circle, 'Worthy is
the Lamb who was slain to receive power and wealth and
wisdom and might and honour and glory and blessing!'[5]

The worship of heaven is thus pictured as being man's
response to God's twofold revelation of himself as Creator and
as Redeemer. In a recent book, Archdeacon Michael Perry has
suggested that the idea of worship is best understood when we
hold in tension the divine prevenience and the human
response:[6] certainly both are important, and we can only
respond to God as he has made himself known to us (cf 2 Cor.
4:6).

In the same book[7] Perry draws attention to the danger of
judging an act of worship by one's answer to the question
'What have I learnt today?' rather than seeking to gain from it
'a sense of the wonder, the joy and the mystery of God'.[8]
Again, these two aims need not necessarily be polarised.
Learning more of the wonderful truths of the Gospel can be a
way of entering into that sense. Martin Bucer in his Censura[9]
wrote that 'the purpose of all the church's observances is the
effective building up of faith in Christ', and in his Preface to the
Book of Common Prayer of 1549, Thomas Cranmer stated of
the divine service that 'the same was not ordeyned, but of a
good purpose, and for a great aduancement of godlines', that
the ministers should 'be stirred up to godlines themselfes . . .'
and that the people 'should continuallye profite more and
more in the knowledge of God, and bee the more inflamed with
the loue of his true religion [sic].'[10] The Reformers were well
aware of the dangers of superstition that had crept in through
the excesses and errors of medieval religion, and were determined to leave no room for misinterpretation.

There are then two great purposes in all our acts of worship

– to glorify God and to edify those taking part – and both have been the manifest concern of those who have been entrusted with the composition or revision of liturgies since the Reformation.

The Danger of a Distorted Emphasis

The Benedictines have a fine phrase for their worship: it is the *opus Dei*, the work of God. Its very ambiguity makes the phrase more meaningful: it is God's work to kindle the desire to worship him in our hearts, and it is our work for God as we respond to him. In Greek the word *leitourgia* came to be used of the worship service. This term had originally been used in classical times to refer to the services that the well-to-do and public-spirited came to perform for the State and their fellows.

Against the background of such connotations (and the fact that we all still have a fallen, even if redeemed-and-being-renewed nature) it is not surprising that in medieval times many churchmen should have regarded services of worship as something they were doing for God, and that

late medieval religion had seemed to the Reformers to be in some of its aspects nothing more than a vast machine for clocking up merit with God, an elaborate means of pulling wires with God, whether through masses or pilgrimages, or invocation of highly-placed saints. Indeed, the whole chantry system looked like a well-organised and sophisticated mechanism for nagging God, motivated by an all-pervading anxiety about whether God really should or would or could grant salvation to the individual.[11]

The Mass had, in fact, come to be regarded as a sacrifice for sinners which the priest was enabled by the grace of orders to offer to God, and this reverses the whole biblical concept of the sacrament, making it an activity which moves from man to God rather than from God to man. The Reformers' understanding is summed up by recent words of Bryan Spinks:

Luther believed the Gospel to be a declaration of the love and forgiveness of God – of what God had done for us. The canon (of the Roman mass), however, is preoccupied with what we are doing for God. It was precisely this which meant that the canon was incompatible with the doctrine of justification.[12]

In consequence, Luther preferred to call the Lord's Supper a testament of forgiveness, and repudiated everything in the canon which smacked of sacrifice.

On the positive side the Anglican reformers defined the sacraments in manward terms:

Sacraments ordained of Christ be not only badges or tokens of Christian men's profession, but rather they be certain sure witnesses and effectual signs of grace, and God's good will towards us, by the which He doth work invisibly in us, and doth not only quicken, but also strengthen and confirm our Faith in Him (Article 25).

Cranmer, in his *Defence of the True and Catholic Doctrine of the Sacrament of the Body and Blood of our Saviour Christ*, wrote (Book V, chap. 10) 'Christ ... ordained them [the sacraments] for this intent, that every man should receive them for himself, to ratify, confirm and stablish his own faith and everlasting salvation.'

It is consonant with this understanding of the use of the sacraments that in the 1549 service of Holy Communion, God is thanked that he has:

assured us (duly receiving the same) of Thy favour and goodness towards us, and that we be very membres incorporate in Thy Misticall bodye, which is the blessed companye of all faythfull people, and heyres through hope of Thy everlasting Kingdome, by the merits of the most precious death and passion, of Thy deare sonne [*sic*].

The revision of 1552 makes the link even clearer by replacing the bracketed phrase with 'thereby', referring back to the earlier words in the prayer which speak of being fed, by duly receiving these holy mysteries, with the spiritual food of the most precious body and blood of our Saviour Jesus Christ.

This accords with the robust assurance of the New Testament, which regards the Christian's right standing before God as assured through faith in Christ Jesus and sealed by the work of the indwelling Holy Spirit.[13] On this understanding of the sacrament of the Lord's Supper the believer can echo the words of the old hymn-writer:

> I hear the words of love,
> I gaze upon the blood,
> I see the mighty sacrifice,
> And I have peace with God.[14]

Objections are sometimes made to this doctrine of assurance because, it is thought, it is presumptuous. That allegation is itself based on a false premise. It would be presumptuous for me to claim assurance of salvation if that salvation depended on my good works or religious observances – but it does not! Since my salvation stems solely from the work of the Lord Jesus Christ in dying for my sins on the cross, and since in the Lord's Supper I am demonstrating my acceptance of that wonderful fact with my heart and mind as I receive the symbols of his broken body and outpoured blood with my mouth, there is no presumption involved. My response is an expression of sheer gratitude, and is the very reverse of claiming to be good enough for God. Only Christ is that, and in baptism and Eucharist, rightly received, the Christian humbly thanks God for being chosen and called to be found the righteousness of God in Christ.[15]

This point is well taken up by Professor Richard Hanson, as follows:

Luther had grasped a great truth which has not been sufficiently understood by many since his day. If we take seriously the witness of the New Testament to the significance and effect of Christ's life and death and resurrection, to the presence of the Holy Spirit and to the situation and prospects of believing Christians, then the idea that religion in any sense at all means an anxious nagging at God becomes impossible ... It is no use nagging at God asking Him to save you because you have in yourself no inducements that can possibly persuade God to save you. And anyway it is perfectly unnecessary to nag, because God has, independently of your anxiety, gratuitously, unexpectedly and inexplicably, given you everything in the way of salvation that you could possibly want in Christ ... Sacrifice therefore becomes something which God graciously gives man, not something which man anxiously offers God.[16]

Three Basic Principles

Considerations such as these led the Reformers on the Continent and in Britain to carry out their work with three basic principles in mind.

1   Liturgical forms are for those who are justified by faith

The basic assumption that all worshippers are believers underlies the whole tenor of Anglican prayer-books. That can be seen in any of the prayer-books in use in the different provinces of the Anglican Communion. In the Church of England's Alternative Service Book, this comes out immediately in the introduction to morning or evening prayer, where the minister may begin, 'We have come together as the family of God in our Father's presence ...'. Prayer-book collects express fully Christian aspirations, and this reflects the same perspective as Paul demonstrated in his letter to the Corinthians, when, for all their faults, he referred to them as 'called to be saints' (1 Cor. 1:2).

While the Christian hope is written into all the prayer-book services, the place where it becomes most apparent is, as we would expect, in the funeral service. The collects written by the Reformers express this hope categorically. There is no place left for prayers for the dead because the believer has no need of them, and the unbeliever is beyond them. So the third part of the Homily on prayer says:

> Now to entreat of that question, Whether we ought to pray for them that are departed out of this world, or no? Wherein, if we will cleave only unto the word of God, then we must needs grant, that we have no commandment so to do . . . let us not deceive ourselves, thinking that either we may help other, or other may help us by their good and charitable prayers in time to come. For . . . every mortal man dieth either in the state of salvation or damnation, according as the words of the evangelist John do [also] plainly import, saying, 'He that believeth on the Son of God hath eternal life: but he that believeth not on the Son, shall never see life, but the wrath of God abideth upon him.'

Here, therefore, as in all other places, the prayer-books of our communion provide a vehicle for worship on the part of those who know themselves to be children of God, members of Christ and inheritors of the kingdom of heaven: in other words, for believers, justified through faith in Jesus Christ their Saviour.

2 Liturgical forms must express Gospel truth

The principle on which our Anglican Reformers worked was that wherever the old forms of service were consistent with 'true setting forth of Christ's religion' (see Cranmer's Preface 'Of Ceremonies, why some be abolished and some retained', which is well worth reading on this point), these forms should be retained. Where, however, they departed from Gospel truth, they were revised as radically as was necessary to bring them into line with clear biblical teaching.

Three examples will show areas in which the Reformers found this to be important. Firstly, in the baptismal service, they saw need to make plain that administration of the sacrament had no *ex opere operato* automatic effect on the recipient. The baptism is followed by a prayer for the infant to experience all that the sacrament has symbolised, and the godparents are reminded of their duty to see that the subject is duly instructed in the beliefs and practice of the Christian faith in order that in due time they may come to confirmation and there ratify the promises that have been made for them. Similarly, the Church of England's Alternative Service Book says, in the introductory statement of its baptismal service:

> Children who are too young to profess the Christian faith are baptised on the understanding that they are brought up as Christians within the family of the Church.
> As they grow up, they need the help and encouragement of that family, so that they learn to be faithful in public worship and private prayer, to live by trust in God, and come to confirmation.

Secondly, as we shall see in greater detail later, the Reformers saw the importance of making the Holy Communion a genuine *eucharistia* – a thanksgiving for the mighty acts of God in Christ. This meant that once the communicants had been reminded of the Lord's institution of the Supper, the most important thing for them to do was to respond to the command to 'Do this in remembrance of me'. And in Reformation thinking, the very act of *anamnesis*, the remembrance of Jesus, was located in their acting out the invitation to 'take and eat this, and drink this, in remembrance' that Christ died, his blood was shed, for them. This is made very clear in the 1662 words of administration, which took their present form in Elizabeth's Prayer Book of 1559. As Spinks again puts it with regard to Luther's reforms, 'Luther's reformed canon replaced "We do" with "He has done";'[17] to which gestures of grateful appropriation are the only fit response.

Our third point concerns the ordinal. The medieval formula

at the ordination of priests was 'Receive thou power to offer sacrifices to God, and to celebrate masses for the living and the dead'. The ordinand was then presented with a paten and chalice as the badges of his office, and vested in the chasuble with the words '*Accipe vestem sacerdotalem*' – receive the garment of a (sacrificing) priest.

The Reformers saw that this concept of priesthood cut clean across the doctrine of justification by faith. Therefore they simplified the words to a receiving of the Holy Spirit for the office and work of a priest in the Church of God, and drew attention to the heart of the presbyteral role by presenting the candidate with a Bible to demonstrate his function as a minister of the Word and a preacher of the Gospel.

3   Liturgical forms must emphasise the centrality of Christ

This is seen in the formularies of the Reformation, which make frequent reference in their texts to our Lord, his person and his work. The writer is reminded of an occasion when, as chaplain of London's Brompton Hospital, he was called on to minister to two patients from overseas, a Lutheran from Iceland and a Coptic Christian from Egypt. Both had expressed a desire for Holy Communion but neither spoke a word of English. As the words of the Book of Common Prayer were read, beams were exchanged every time the name of 'Jesus Christ' was mentioned – and there were a good many beams.

But it is not simply in the words that Christ must be central. The medieval church was rich in symbolism, and there is a strong desire today to restore this emphasis. Some symbolism can be helpful: for instance, the cruciform layout of many churches, which can be achieved even where the building is rectangular by the traditional Anglican arrangement of:

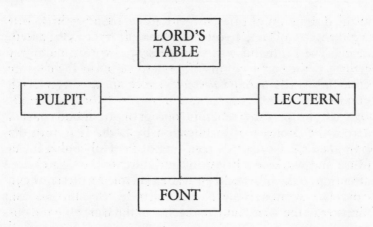

This demonstrates on its two axes the unity of the ministry of Word and sacrament and is a powerful reminder of the centrality of the cross. A cross or other Christian symbol, or a Christocentric text above the Lord's table, can also be a powerful and evocative focal point. But we must beware lest we open the door too widely and reintroduce the state of things against which the Reformers had to react. In a recent book Bishop Michael Marshall refers to this danger when he writes:

... sometimes ceremonial, signs and symbols are counterproductive because they draw attention away from God by focusing on themselves. Symbolism can become obscured and tamed by aesthetic considerations until it reaches the point where it actually distracts from the message which it is seeking to convey. So it was that by the fifteenth century the ceremonies of the Church in the West had become so decadent that it was scarcely possible to see through them: the icon had become an idol; the means had become an end. It was against that background that the Puritans became so iconoclastic, seeking to tear down all that hindered plain speaking.[18]

Our Reformers saw danger in the symbolism of the priest at Holy Communion standing in the so-called 'Eastward position' between the people and the place where it had been taught that God would 'presence himself', and so they relocated him at the North side of the table. Today the rediscovery of the primitive use of the 'Westward position', where the presiding minister faces the people across the table, is proving a unitive feature in ecumenical liturgy. At the same time, however, we may well ask whether Cranmer did not have a wise insight in moving the minister(s) to the side in order to leave the central position empty for the visibly-absent yet spiritually-present-to-the-eye-of-faith Lord of the Church.

Similarly, the Reformers' insistence, made clear in the 1552 prayer-book, subsequently reinforced by the Elizabethan Advertisements, and followed in the Church of England for 300 years, that ministers should wear the same vesture at all times of their ministration, demonstrated symbolically the unity of the ministry of Word and sacrament. If the Church continues the use of robes in worship, for which there are still strong arguments, we need to ask ourselves whether a more elaborate vesture for some services than others may not introduce an unbiblical element of 'double-think' into our attitudes to those services, leading us to regard the sacrament as more important than the Word.

It was in the service of Holy Communion that the Reformers sought most of all to express these newly-rediscovered doctrines of the Bible, and to this service we must now turn.

Cranmer's Communion Service

It was precisely because he had grasped the point that salvation is entirely the work of a justifying God, and wished to maintain the principles stated above, that Cranmer treated the liturgy of the Lord's Supper as he did in his Prayer-Book of 1552. There he reconstructed the canon of the Mass in such a way that God's movement of grace towards man, with the anamnesis of the finished work of Christ followed by the words of institution, dominates the prayer of consecration. Demonstrating their obedience to the command to 'do this in remembrance of me' the communicants then at once came forward to take, eat and drink, and only after that climactic action[19] did the movement of the service take the opposite direction, that of self-giving to God as distinct from receiving from God. Man's response, verbalised in the post-communion prayers of all Anglican liturgies, is to offer himself in response to the amazing grace which the sacrament proclaims, and to make the sacrifice for which God looks – that of the broken spirit, now healed and restored and ready to express gratitude for all God has done for us in Christ. As the former vice-principal of Oak Hill, Alan Stibbs, never tired of repeating,

> I could not work my soul to save,
> For that my Lord has done;
> But I will work like any slave
> For love of God's dear Son!

Man's response to God's grace can only be to come with open hand to receive what God has to offer: in Toplady's words –

> Nothing in my hand I bring
> Simply to Thy cross I cling . . .[20]

Any emphasis on the human part at this stage would invite the criticism Michael Ramsey[21] levels at the introduction of the offertory procession, so popular among the supporters of the Parish Communion movement, as being 'a shallow and romantic form of semi-Pelagianism'.

Modern Understandings

Cranmer's structure breathes a different atmosphere from that of the recent ARCIC statement, which appears to try to combine both these approaches in a remarkably ambiguous manner:

There is therefore, one historical, unrepeatable sacrifice, offered once for all by Christ and accepted once for all by the Father. In the celebration of the memorial, Christ in the Holy Spirit unites His people with Himself in a sacramental way so that the Church enters into the movement of His self-offering. In consequence, even though the Church is active in this celebration, this adds nothing to the efficacy of Christ's sacrifice upon the cross, because the action is itself the fruit of the sacrifice. The Church in celebrating the Eucharist gives thanks for the gift of Christ's sacrifice, and identifies itself with the will of Christ who has offered Himself to the Father on behalf of all mankind.[22]

The idea that Christ is perpetually offering himself to the Father, and that this is an activity into which the Church enters in the Eucharist, is extremely popular in modern theology. In Anglican circles it has been particularly in fashion since the Lambeth Conference of 1958 when the appropriate committee quoted with favour some words of Dr A. G. Hebert highlighting the idea that Christian people participate by the Eucharist in Christ's action of offering himself.[23]

Those who follow Hebert's line of thinking base their theories of Christ's present offering on the imagery of the Epistle to the Hebrews, especially chapter 8, verse 3, but this position was earlier considered in some detail by Dr A. J. Tait in his *Heavenly Session of our Lord*,[24] and shown to be mistaken. A simple reading of the New Testament shows that Jesus, at the moment of his death, was aware that he had finished the reconciling work he had come to do, and that on entering heaven he was assigned the seat of honour at the right hand of the Father, since his work on Calvary was now complete. His offering of himself on the cross was accepted by the Father at the time it was made, and the enthroning of the ascended Son proclaims this to be so. As Bishop Westcott wrote in his commentary on the Epistle to the Hebrews:

The modern conception of Christ pleading in heaven His Passion, 'Offering His Blood', on behalf of men, has no foundation in the Epistle. His glorified humanity is the eternal pledge of the absolute efficacy of His accomplished work. He pleads, as older writers truly expressed the thought, by His Presence on the Father's Throne.[25]

In a more recent commentary on Hebrews, P. E. Hughes devotes an excursus of some twenty-five pages to the question of the blood of Jesus and his heavenly priesthood, in which he reaches the conclusion:

The intercession of the Son, then, is in no sense a pleading with the Father to change his attitude toward us. Nor does the Father have to be reminded of the full redemption that he himself has provided for us in his Son – the very thought is preposterous! The presence in heaven of the Lamb bearing the marks of his passion is itself the perpetual guarantee of our acceptance with God, who gave his Son to be the propitiation for our sins. In ourselves, however, though we have the forgiveness of our sins through the blood of Jesus Christ and though we are united to him in love and trust, we are unworthy because Christ has not yet been fully formed within us (cf Gal. 4:19) and we still sinfully fall short of the glory of God (cf Rom. 3:23). This consideration explains our continuing need of the advocacy and intercession of him who alone is accounted worthy before God (cf Rev. 5:1–10). It is in his worthiness that even now we rejoice in the blessing of the divine favor, for by the grace of God his merit has been reckoned to us as our merit, his heaven has become our heaven, and his eternal glory our eternal glory.[26]

The Modern Dilemma

We noticed earlier that Dix praised Cranmer for producing a communion service that clearly expressed the doctrine of justification by faith. That is important, but we also need to ask the question whether that should be the sole purpose of a eucharistic liturgy, or whether other concerns need to be borne in mind.

Most Anglicans would feel that they do. While it was right at the Reformation that this doctrine should be to the fore, so that worshippers should be left in no doubt as to the only grounds upon which a sinful man can approach a holy God, four centuries of using what was essentially Cranmer's service (for the 1662 revision left it almost untouched) did breed a very individualistic type of communicant ('I come to make my communion' – clergy who ministered before Series 2 hit us will be familiar with this person). Modern writers and liturgies have encouraged us to see that, while the backward look to Calvary should be pre-eminent at the Lord's Supper, there is also a place for the upward look to the risen and ascended Lord as he is known to us in the breaking of bread, the outward look to my neighbour (be he or she in or out of church), and the forward look to the coming of the Lord, for the Lord's Supper is an interim rite only to be observed 'till He come'.[27] As the welcoming words carved in the oak panelling behind the Lord's table in East Barnet parish church remind us, 'Blessed are those who are called to the marriage-supper of the Lamb',[28] and the Lord's Supper is a sign and seal to the believer that he or she is so called.

Losing the Biblical Baby with the Medieval Bathwater

What we are saying therefore is that we needed the modern revisions of the liturgy and can rejoice in the wider perspectives they give us. Sometimes, too, they confirm the historic evangelical emphases in helpful ways. The very doctrine we are now considering is verbalised in one of the Rite A alternative forms introducing the peace: Cranmer would surely have seen 'being justified by faith, we have peace with God' as a very 'comfortable word' leading in to the thanksgiving. Again the alternative form of post-communion thanksgiving highlights a Gospel picture that is not found in the Book of Common Prayer – 'when we were still far off you met us in your Son and brought us home'.

This is all gain, and we should not wish to put the clock back

on the progress of revision. However, there is a sense in which
the clock has already been put back for us by those who have
preferred a 1549 type of structure for the eucharistic canon to
that of 1552, particularly in respect of expressing the concept
that the worshippers make some form of offering to God
before they receive. This particular swing of the pendulum has
a long history, via the Laudian liturgy of 1637, the Scottish
liturgy of 1764 and that version subsequently exported via
Samuel Seabury to the Episcopal Church of the USA.[29]

Attention was drawn to this fact in the 1958 Lambeth
Conference report, which quoted Dr Massey Shepherd's well-
known words: 'Our Communion, with its two types of liturgy,
expressive of two approaches to the problem (of the Eucharistic Sacrifice) may be able to hold its various facets in tension.
Sooner or later, however, it must be resolved.'[30] The present
trend is that we are moving back in the majority of our
alternative forms of liturgy to the 1549 structure, with Series 1,
all four of the Rite A eucharistic prayers, and Rite B in the
Alternative Service Book, giving us a 1549 pattern of focusing
on what we are now doing at the very point in the service
where exponents of justification by faith wish to see the
emphasis on what God in Christ has done. Spinks sees Luther
in his *Deutsche Messe* of 1526 anticipating what Cranmer was
to do twenty-six years later by removing any such emphasis, as
we have noted above.[31]

Evidence that this trend is not confined to churches of the
Anglican Communion is found in the recent publication of the
so-called Lima liturgy, which reached the limelight when it
was used by the Archbishop of Canterbury at the Vancouver
Assembly of the World Council of Churches in 1983.[32] Here
the words of institution and the actual communion are separated by no less than nine paragraphs. The first of them,
entitled 'Anamnesis' contains the declaration 'United in
Christ's priesthood, we present to you this memorial: Remem-
ber the sacrifice of your Son . . .' Such an emphasis, coming at
this point in the service, calls for Luther's comment, 'with
unheard of perversity, we mock at the mercy of the Giver; for
we give as a work what we should be accepting as a gift, till the

Testator now no longer distributes the largesse of His own good things, but becomes the recipient of ours. Alas for such a sacrilege!'[33]

In a subsequent section (28, The peace) the man-centred rather than God-centred emphasis is maintained by the phrase 'Look not on our sins but on the faith of your Church'. This is a confusing idea, and many Christians would prefer to see some such wording as 'Look not on our sins but on the work of your Son'. We obviously still have some distance to go in the quest for an ecumenical liturgy that will do justice to the insights of the Reformers.

A Plea for 1990

While we have readily admitted that there are other emphases besides justification by faith which we should wish to see in our communion service, the good news of forgiveness through Christ's cross must always be the dominant theme in eucharistic worship. For it is here that we 'shew the Lord's death'[34] and are reminded of the earliest Christian tradition that 'Christ died for our sins in accordance with the scriptures, that he was buried, that he was raised on the third day in accordance with the scriptures and that he appeared . . .'[35]

Any feature which would detract from the completeness of our salvation in Christ or rob the Christian of his or her birthright of assurance must be resisted as strongly as the Reformers did. So R. J. Coates wrote,

> modern re-interpretations of the movement of the Eucharist which make our self-sacrifice with Christ mystical precede our reception of the sacrament of Christ personal and present, not only forsake the order of salvation, but open the door to the lamentable errors which our forefathers excluded so effectively in the sixteenth century.

Such doctrine in effect turns saving faith into a saving work, and implies that the direct ground on which eternal life is given us is our own active self-sacrifice. We must beware of teaching which seems to imply that the Church in union with Christ saves itself by its act of offering, and does not make clear that the Church is saved by Christ alone, through faith alone, on the ground of his blood and righteousness alone.

The glory of the Triune God is the end of our existence, and must always be the object of all our life and teaching. We must hold, then, to a theology which will preserve the glory of Christ, and not take from it. No man can offer Christ. There is a sense in which we can plead His merit, claiming Him as our propitiation and Advocate with God, but it is not for us to offer Him to God, and so obscure the glory of His perfect finished work. No man can offer with Christ, that is, placing himself alongside Christ; we offer ourselves to God through Christ, but our offering depends upon His, and is not to be confused with it. Let us learn to place our emphasis in our expression of saving truth in the place where the Eternal Son is most gloriously revealed. Let us glory always and only in the Cross of Christ. Let us learn to sing on earth the song of heaven, 'Worthy is the Lamb that was slain'.[36]

We need a return to Cranmer's clarity of language (albeit in contemporary terms) and to his structure when we come to revise the Alternative Service Book in 1990. If we wish to say anything in the eucharistic prayer about what we are doing (which is not really necessary, unless we are totally bemused by Hippolytus and the other primitive liturgies), let us follow the wise example of Series 3 and be neither more nor less ambiguous than the plain words of the New Testament – '. . . we do this in remembrance of him . . .'

How we do this then needs to be explained to the modern worshipper as clearly as the Reformers did in the Book of Common Prayer. There is a place in the Alternative Service Book for the type of exhortation/explanation the Reformers provided, especially for those congregations and individuals who may never see or hear the Book of Common Prayer (and

already a significant proportion of such people are now entering our theological colleges). As an introduction to the liturgy
of the upper room, Cranmer provided an explanation of
remembrance and thanksgiving at the end of his first exhortation of 1549 (moved to third place in 1552) as follows:

> ... to the end that we should alway remember the exceed-
> ing great love of our Master and only Saviour Jesus Christ,
> thus dying for us, and the innumerable benefits which by His
> precious blood-shedding He hath obtained to us; he hath
> instituted and ordained holy mysteries as pledges of His love,
> and for a continual remembrance of His death, to our great
> and endless comfort.

There remains a place for such explanation.

In his chapter on the Orthodox understanding of this subject
Gerald Bray[37] has drawn attention to the way in which Eastern
theology, and therefore liturgy, has seen salvation as effected
through the whole process of 'incarnation-leading-to-
atonement'. This to Western ears appears to over-emphasise
the Incarnation, which the biblical record presents as the
necessary way for 'God-to-become-man-in-order-to-die'.

While there is a sense in which it is artificial to separate the
various stages of the total cycle of the Incarnation-life-
ministry-passion-death-resurrection-ascension-coming-again
of our Lord Jesus, the biblical writers are unequivocal in laying
stress on the fact that the problem of sin and man's relation
with a holy God through justification could only be dealt with
by the death of Jesus on the cross. 'As often as you eat this
bread and drink the cup, you proclaim the Lord's *death* until
He comes . . .'[38] is the Pauline charter for those who would
revise the service of the Lord's Supper. In the face of theologies
which would relate this service to the Incarnation rather than
the Atonement we cannot emphasise this fact too strongly.

For those who would appreciate an alternative to an updat-
ing of 1662, but recognise the importance of retaining the
traditional Western emphasis on the uniqueness of the Atonement, there is still scope for imaginative revision. The Anglican

Church of Chile published a revision in 1973, which has been much appreciated, when it has been used in Oak Hill chapel on an experimental basis, for the way it handles the recitation of the facts of our salvation with biblical reference. Here the prayer labelled 'Consecration' (would it today be called 'Thanksgiving'?) reads:

> Glory be to you, almighty God, our heavenly Father, because in your great mercy you delivered up your only son Jesus Christ to suffer death upon the cross for our redemption. He was offered once for all time, and made there a single, perfect and sufficient sacrifice and propitiation for the sins of the whole world. He was wounded for our transgressions, he was bruised for our iniquities; the punishment for our peace was upon him, and with his stripes we are healed. All we like sheep have gone astray, but you have laid on him the sin of us all.
> Worthy is the Lamb who was slain;
> To him who sits upon the throne and to the Lamb
> be the praise, and honour, the glory, and the power,
> for ever and ever. Amen.
> We also give you thanks, merciful Father, that our Lord Jesus instituted this sacrament and commanded us to continue it until his coming again. He, in the same night that he was betrayed, took bread, and having given thanks, broke it and said: 'Take, eat; this is my body which is given for you. Do this in remembrance of me.' In the same way, after supper he took the cup and said: 'This cup is the new covenant in my blood. Do this as often as you drink it in remembrance of me.'
> Christ, we proclaim your death, we confess your resurrection, we look for your coming. Glory be to you. Amen.[39]

The distribution of the elements follows immediately.

The writer of the Epistle to the Hebrews[40] urges Christian people to approach God's throne with boldness – the Greek word literally means in a state of being able to tell him everything. The evangelical attitude to revised liturgy has in the early stages been a defensive one of fighting a rearguard action in order to preserve the doctrinal emphases of 1662. That approach will no longer do. As we prepare for 1990 and further revision (or a move to perpetuate what we have now settled for in Rites A and B as the established alternatives – assuming that Series 2 and 3 will be allowed to lapse in 1985) we need to start from a different position.

The cardinal doctrine of justification by faith needs restatement in vigorous, positive and simple terms so that the man on the Clapham bus (the twentieth-century equivalent of Tyndale's man following the plough) will understand and respond. When he comes into our churches (and please God some of the evangelistic efforts now taking place will bring in many such), he must find a liturgy of the Lord's Supper which will match his experience and be a meaningful expression of *eucharistia*, thanksgiving, for his experience of the mighty acts of God in Christ for his salvation. It is our prayer that this book will be a step on the way by preparing its readers, and especially the clergy and others involved in contemporary Christian ministry, for their part in this task.

NOTES

1. Justification in the Old Testament

1 In Gen. 20:16 the word *kᵉsût* (RSV vindication) usually meaning 'covering'; it is of little interest for our subject.

2 E.g. R. Kittel, (ed), *Theological Dictionary of the New Testament*, (10 vols), Eng. trans. (Eerdmans, 1964–76); C. Brown (ed), *New International Dictionary of New Testament Theology*, (3 vols), (Paternoster, 1975–8); G. A. Buttrick, (ed), *Interpreter's Dictionary of the Bible*, (4 vols plus Supplement), (Abingdon, 1962, 1976); J. D. Douglas and N. Hillyer, (edd), *Illustrated Bible Dictionary*, (3 vols), (IVP, 1980); G. W. Bromiley, (ed), *International Standard Bible Encyclopedia*, (4 vols), (Eerdmans, 1979–); G. J. Botterweck and H. Ringgren, (edd), *Theological Dictionary of the Old Testament*, (10 vols), Eng. trans. (Eerdmans, 1977–), etc.

3 *Die paulinische Rechtfertigungslehre im Zusammenhange ihrer geschichtlichen Voraussetzungen.*

4 W. Eichrodt, *Theology of the Old Testament*, vol 1 (SCM, 1961), p 240.

5 E.g. W. Eichrodt, G. von Rad, W. Zimmerli, *et al.* See also E. R. Achtemeier, 'Righteousness in the OT' in *Interpreter's Dictionary of the Bible*.

6 *Die Derivate des Stammes im alttestamentlichen Sprachgebrauch*, 1881; followed by E. Jacob, *Theology of the Old Testament*, Eng. trans. (Hodder & Stoughton, 1958); also earlier by N. H. Snaith, *Distinctive Ideas of the Old Testament*, (Epworth, 1944).

7 *Op. cit*, pp. 83, 85.

8 *hiphil.*

9 The words translated 'condemning' and 'guilty' are from the

same root: 'pronouncing the wicked to be wicked' as with 'justifying the just'.

10 See also Job 33:32; Jer. 3:11; Ezek. 16:51f (all *piel*). The non-causative form (*qal*) of the verb occurs sometimes with the meaning 'be justified', e.g. Isa. 43:9, 26. The reflexive (*hithpael*) occurs once, Gen. 44:16 meaning 'show ourselves to be righteous'.

11 The verb used is *he²emîn*, the *hiphil* of *²āmēn*, 'to be firm'. It is found in several constructions: on its own; followed by an accusative; or by *b^e*, meaning 'in', or by *l^e*, meaning 'to'. Both *b^e* and *l^e* can be used with a direct object under certain circumstances; or followed by 'that ...' or by an infinitive. See Botterweck and Ringgren, *op. cit.*, vol 1, pp. 298–309.

12 Cf also Jer. 12:6; 40:14; 2 Chr. 32:15; 1 Kgs. 10:7 and Isa. 53 (reports); Prov. 26:25. It does not seem possible to make a clear distinction between the usage with *b^e* and *l^e*. Those with Hebrew may find the most convenient way of checking in G. Lisowsky, *Kondordanz zum Hebräischen Alten Testament* (Würtembergische Bibelanstalt, Stuttgart, 1958).

13 *²āman* in Botterweck etc., *op. cit.*, p. 308.

14 The rendering 'strengthened himself in Yahweh' is plausible etymologically, but this is a most uncertain way of deciding on the meaning of a word. We communicate by using words in the way our readers/hearers understand them.

15 We might perhaps distinguish between belief and profession. The problem is that whatever words we use are open to ambiguity and misunderstanding.

16 'Faith Reckoned as Righteousness' (1951), in *The Problem of the Hexateuch*, Eng. trans. (Oliver and Boyd, 1966), pp. 125–30.

17 Most recently by C. Westermann, *Biblischer Kommentar altes Testament 1, 14 Genesis 14:1–17:27* (Neukirchen-Vluyn, 1979), pp. 263f.

18 'Genesis 15:6 im Neuen Testament' in the Festschrift for G. von Rad, 1971. Quoted in C. Westermann, *op. cit.*, p. 248.

19 See their respective commentaries on Romans 1:17 (and J. B. Lightfoot on Gal. 3:11).

20 *op. cit.* (Zondervan Edition, 1962), p. 155.

21 Hebrew *tāmîm*, complete, whole, mature.

22 Gen. 6:9(P), cf 7:1(J).

23 Gen. 6:8(J).

24 Gen. 12:1–3.

25 Gen. 20:4–6, 9f.
26 Many scholars see deuteronomic influence in 22:15–18; 26:2–5.
27 Gen. 30:35f.; 31:5–12, 36–42.
28 Gen. 28:11–17.
29 Gen. 39:21–3; 40:8; 41:16, 25, 28, 32; 41:38f.; 41:51f.; 46:1–3; 50:24f.; 42:28; 44:16; 45:5, 7, 8, 9.
30 Exod. 3:11, 13; 4:1, 10, 13.
31 Perhaps striking the rock twice is meant to emphasise this somewhat arrogant attitude.
32 It is quite difficult to find Old Testament examples of this; see 1 Sam. 16:7; 13:14 below, and Jer. 29:13. Cornelius springs to mind from the New Testament.
33 Judg. 4:9.
34 Judg. 6:15, 27, 36–40; 6:12, 16.
35 Judg. 7:4–7, 9, 14. The drinking method probably does not imply any special qualities. The purpose of the test is simply to whittle down the numbers so that the Lord may be glorified, and be more obviously the One who gives the victory.
36 Judg. 16:30. We may doubt the depth of theological understanding expressed in his prayer (v. 28). It probably has something to teach us about answers to our own at times pathetic prayers.
37 1 Sam. 9:21, 23.
38 cf 15:28 'a neighbour of yours who is better than you'.
39 1 Sam. 15:30. Saul, of course, is not cut off from his people, nor even deposed, but his descendants do not succeed to the throne.
40 E.g. 1 Kgs. 15:3–5.
41 See e.g. R. T. France, *Jesus and the Old Testament*, (IVP, 1971).
42 E.g. 9:6, 13.
43 Rom. 3:8; 6:2–4.
44 cf Jer. 29:13.
45 Job 9:2, cf 12:3b and possibly 9:14f., 19f., 28–33; cf also Ps. 143:1f. above.
46 Rom. 10:5.
47 *Isaiah 40–66 (New Century Bible)*, (Oliphants, 1975); also *Thanksgiving of a Liberated Prophet*, (Almond, 1981).
48 C. R. North, *The Suffering Servant in Deutero–Isaiah* (Oxford, 1948), pp. 226f.
49 Esp. Zech. 12:10–13:1; 13:7–9.

2. Righteousness by faith in the New Testament

1 Quoted from the edition of the *Homilies* by G. E. Corrie, (Cambridge, 1850), p. 19.

2 The uncertainty arises from the uncertain text at Matt. 27:4.

3 B. Przybylski, *Righteousness in Matthew and his World of Thought*, (Cambridge, 1980).

4 It must be admitted that this interpretation of Matthew 3:15 and 21:23 is by no means widely supported. Przybylski *op. cit.*, pp. 91–6 provides a brief summary of opinions. His own view is that both verses refer merely to the righteousness demanded of men in accordance with God's will. But this seems so bland as to rob Matthew 3:15 of all real significance. It goes without saying that Jesus and John must obey the will of God: why should such a commonplace be given such pivotal importance at Jesus' baptism? The strange thing is that Przybylski, having rightly maintained that the Old Testament represents an essential point of departure for Matthew's view of righteousness (pp. 8–12), then ignores the vital Old Testament use of the word to signify God's *saving* righteousness, which can be shown to underlie all uses of the term in the Old Testament (see E. Achtemeier, 'Righteousness in the OT', *Interpreter's Dictionary of the Bible*, (Nashville, 1962) vol. 4, pp. 80–5) and must have conditioned Matthew's instinctive understanding of the word.

5 For an exposition of the relationship between election and law in the Judaism of Paul's day, a now indispensable book is E. P. Sanders's *Paul and Palestinian Judaism*, (London, 1977).

6 The interpretation of Romans 7 has been exhaustively surveyed and assessed by Peter Pytches in a Dissertation for which he was awarded a Doctorate while on the staff of Oak Hill College: P. N. L. Pytches, *The Interpretation of Romans 7:14–25*, (Diss, Southampton, 1981).

7 C. E. B. Cranfield, 'St Paul and the Law', in R. Batey (ed), *New Testament Issues*, (London, 1970), pp. 148–72; here, pp. 152–3.

8 We find, for instance, the following statement in the Mishnah (Yoma 8:8): 'Repentance works atonement for light offences against commands and prohibitions; in the case of serious offences repentance works postponement until the Day of Atonement comes and brings expiation'.

9 J. A. Ziesler, *The Meaning of Righteousness in Paul* (Cambridge, 1972). For this distinction, see especially pp. 168–9.

3. Justification by Faith: a truth for our times

1 Luther: Sermon, 25 July, 1522: *WA* (Weimar edition of Luther's works, 1883–) 10:3:239.
2 Hans Küng, *Justification* (Burns Oates, 1964), pp. 238f.
3 On Romans 4:7: *WA* 56:272:17.
4 On Romans 12:2: *WA* 56:442:17.
5 J. Calvin, *Inst* III. xi. 7.
6 T. F. Torrance, *Theology in Reconstruction* (SCM Press, London, 1965), p. 115.
7 *Epistolae M. Lutheri* (Jena, 1556), i. 345.
8 A key sentence in the Tridentine statement on Scripture and tradition was first drafted to say that the truth of Christ is contained *partly* in written books (i.e. Scripture), *partly* in unwritten traditions (*partim . . . partim* in Latin). After opposition in debate from Bonucci and Jacob Nachianti, Bishop of Chioggia, it was changed to read 'in written books *and* (*et*) in unwritten traditions'. Thus the question whether tradition supplements Scripture or only expounds it was left open, though the first draft would have closed it by affirming the first of these options. Following Melchior Cano, Canisius, and Robert Bellarmine, Roman Catholic theologians from the sixteenth to the twentieth century have defended the first option as if Trent had in fact affirmed it; but Vatican II limited itself to spelling out the second, and it seems that most Roman Catholic leaders today embrace that view. For the story of second thoughts at Trent, see J. R. Gieselmann, 'Scripture, Tradition and the Church: an Ecumenical Problem' in *Christianity Divided*, D. J. Callahan, H. A. Obermann, D. J. O'Hanlon (edd), (Sheed and Ward, London and New York, 1962), pp. 39–72, especially pp. 43–8, 65f.; for Trent's final text, see *Enchiridion Symbolorum*, H. Denzinger, C. Bannwart, J. B. Umberg, C. Rahner (edd) (Herder, Freiburg, many editions), No. 783 (Latin), and *The Church Teaches*, J. F. Clarkson, J. H. Edwards, W. J. Kelly, J. J. Welch, (edd), (Herder, St Louis, 1955), pp. 44f. (English).

4. Justification in Protestant theology

1 G. C. Berkouwer, *Faith and Justification* (Eerdmans, Grand Rapids, 1954), p. 17.

2 *Works* (reprinted, Banner of Truth, London), I, 321.

3 'The sum of this epistle is to pull down, and pluck up and destroy, all the wisdom and righteousness of the flesh . . . and to affirm and state and magnify sin.' 'For God wills to save us, not by our own righteousness and wisdom, but by one from without . . . which comes from heaven. Thus it is by all means necessary to learn this external and foreign righteousness: for which reason our own internal righteousness, must be first removed.' Luther, *Works*, J. C. F. Knaske *et al.* (edd), (Weimar, 1883–), LVI 157, 158; from the Lectures on Romans (1515–16).

4 *Tota haec doctrina ad illud certamen perterrefactae conscientiae referanda est, nec sine illo certamine intelligi potest. Quare male judicant de ea re homines imperiti et profani* (Augsburg Confession, XX).

5 The chapter is entitled: 'That we may be thoroughly convinced of free (*gratuita*) justification, we must lift up our mind to God's judgement-seat (*tribunal*).'

6 *Works*, W. H. Goold, (ed), (reprinted, Banner of Truth, London, 1967), V 7, 4.

7 Calvin, *Inst*, III. xi. 2.

8 The title of *Inst*, II. xvii is: 'It is right and proper to say that Christ *merited* God's grace and salvation for us.' So Anglican Article XI affirms: 'We are accounted righteous before God, only for the *merit* of our Lord and Saviour Jesus Christ, by Faith, and not for our own works or deservings.' And the Holy Communion service of the Book of Common Prayer complements this statement when it speaks of Christ as having 'made (by his one oblation of himself once offered) a full, perfect and sufficient sacrifice, oblation and *satisfaction* for the sins of the whole world.'

9 *Works*, V. 608; from the Commentary on the Psalms (1519–21).

10 *Works*, LVI. 347. Elsewhere Luther speaks of the Christian as *simul justus et peccator* – simultaneously righteous through Christ and a sinner in himself – and as *semper peccator, semper penitens, semper justus* (ibid, p. 442).

11 Thus what is satisfied is God's *Law*, not just his *honour*; and the analogy for the transaction shifts from compensation, or damages in a civil suit, to the retributive infliction of penalty in a criminal court.

12 *Galatians*, 1535, ed from the 1575 English translation by Philip S. Watson (James Clarke, London, 1953), pp. 269–71. Galatians was Luther's favourite epistle, and he was pleased with his

commentary on it. When the complete Latin edition of his works was being prepared two years before his death, he said: 'If they took my advice, they'd print only the books containing doctrine, like Galatians' (ibid, p. 5). Gustaf Aulén in chapter VI of *Christus Victor* (SPCK, London, 1931) was right to stress the dynamism of divine victory in Luther's account of the work of Christ, but wrong to ignore the penal substitution in terms of which that work is basically defined. Christ's victory, according to Luther, consisted precisely in the fact that he effectively purged our sins as our substitute on the cross, so freeing us from Satan's power by overcoming God's curse; if Luther's whole treatment of Gal. 3:13 (pp. 268–2) is read, this becomes very plain.

13 Calvin, *Inst*, II. xvi. 5, 7. An excellent book on Calvin's doctrine of the cross is Paul Van Buren, *Christ in Our Place: the substitutionary character of Calvin's doctrine of reconciliation* (Oliver and Boyd, Edinburgh, 1957). Van Buren notes that 'there is no trace of a substitutionary understanding of the trial before Pilate in either (Peter) Lombard or Aquinas', the two most standard medieval theologians (ibid, p. 46, n. 2).

14 *Inst*, II, xvi. 10.

15 Cf Westminster Confession XI.11: 'faith . . . the alone instrument of justification . . . is . . . not alone in the person justified, but is ever accompanied with all other saving graces, and is no dead faith but worketh by love'.

16 'Justification by Faith: the Reinstatement of the Doctrine Today', *Evangelical Quarterly*, July, 1952, p. 166.

17 Among major Reformed treatments of justification (in English) may be mentioned, Owen, op. cit.; Jonathan Edwards, 'Justification By Faith Alone', *Works*, E. Hickman (ed), (reprinted, Banner of Truth, London, 1974), pp. 622–54; J. Buchanan, *The Doctrine of Justification* (reprinted, Banner of Truth, London, 1961); Berkouwer, op. cit.; C. Hodge, *Systematic Theology*, (Nelson, London, 1874), III, 114–212.

18 See the decrees of Trent, Session VI. vii. This doctrine is immediately applied in the unhappy canon 9: 'If any say that the sinner is justified through faith alone, in the sense that nothing else is necessary that co-operates to obtain the grace of justification, and that it is not necessary for the sinner to prepare himself, by means of his own will, let him be anathema.'

19 Cf the remarkable statement of Session V.v: 'Concupiscence, which the Apostle sometimes calls sin, the holy Council declares

that the Catholic Church has never understood to be called sin in the sense that it is truly and properly sin in those born again, but in the sense that it is of sin and inclines to sin. Should anyone be of a contrary opinion, let him be anathema.'

20 Hooker, 'A learned discourse of Justification', *Works*, (Clarendon Press, Oxford, 1865), II.606. Note how heavily Hooker's statement underlines Calvin's basic perspective, that our union with Christ is the foundation of the imputing of his righteousness to us. Owen underlines the same point with equal emphasis.

'The foundation of the imputation is union. Hereof there are many grounds and causes . . . but that which we have immediate respect unto, as the foundation of this imputation, is that whereby the Lord Christ and believers do actually *coalesce into one mystical person*. This is by the Holy Spirit inhabiting in him as the head of the church in all fullness, and in all believers according to their measure, whereby they become members of his mystical body. That there is such a union between Christ and believers is the faith of the catholic church and hath been so in all ages. Those who seem in our days to deny it, or question it, either know not what they say, or their minds are influenced by their doctrine who deny the divine persons of the Son and of the Spirit (i.e., the Socinians). Upon supposition of this union, reason will grant the imputation pleaded for to be reasonable; at least, there is such a peculiar ground for it as is not to be exemplified in any things natural or political among men' (*Works*, V.209).

21 For the generalisations of this section, cf C. F. Allison, *The Rise of Moralism*, (SPCK, London, 1966), passim; Peter Toon, *Justification and Sanctification*, (Marshall, Morgan and Scott, London, 1983), pp. 89–102; R. A. Leaver, *The Doctrine of Justification in the Church of England*, (Latimer House, Oxford, 1979); R. G. England, *Justification Today: The Roman Catholic and Anglican Debate*, (Latimer House, Oxford, 1979); Alister McGrath, 'The Emergence of the Anglican Tradition on Justification, 1600–1700' (*Churchman*, 1984, 98.1, pp. 28–43); ibid, 'ARCIC II and Justification', (*Anvil*, 1984, 1.1, pp. 27–42).

22 *Works*, LACT, (Oxford, 1847–49), I.114.

5. Justification and the Eastern Orthodox Churches

1 Cf C. E. B. Cranfield, *A Critical and Exegetical Commentary on the Epistle to the Romans* (Edinburgh, 1975), vol. 1, pp. 274–9.

2 J. Meyendorff, *Byzantine Theology* (London, 1974), p. 145.

3 Ibid, pp. 160–1.

4 Ibid, p. 160.

5 Cf Cranfield, op. cit., p. 221, n. 3.

6 Meyendorff, op. cit., p. 143.

7 S. Runciman, *The Great Church in Captivity* (Cambridge, 1968), p. 246.

8 The text can be found in I. Karmirēs, *Ta dogmatika kai symbolika mnēmeia tēs orthodoxou katholikēs ecclēsias* (Athēnai, 1960), vol. 1, pp. 432–503.

9 Ibid. The translator was Paul Dolscius of Plauen.

10 J. Pelikan, *The Christian Tradition Vol. 2: The Spirit of Eastern Christendom (600–1700)*, p. 281.

11 Ibid.

12 It is not recorded in classical or patristic literature.

13 As cited by Pelikan, op. cit., p. 285.

14 Ibid.

15 Runciman, op. cit., p. 345.

16 Ibid, p. 350.

17 J. Karmirēs, op. cit., vol. 2, pp. 746–73.

18 Cf V. Lossky, *The Mystical Theology of the Eastern Church* (Cambridge, 1957), and *In the Image and Likeness of God* (London, 1975).

19 V. Lossky, *Orthodox Theology: An Introduction* (Crestwood, New York, 1978), p. 115.

20 Cf Cranfield, op. cit., pp. 274–9; Meyendorff, op. cit., p. 144.

6. Justification and Roman Catholicism
(An essay submitted by the author in Dec 1982)

1 As in the *Anglican–Lutheran International Conversations* (Pullach Report), (SPCK, 1973).

2 A. McGrath, 'Justification: Barth, Trent and Küng', *Scottish Journal of Theology*, vol. 34, No. 6, p. 519.

3 Burns and Oates (London, 1964).

4 McGrath, op. cit., p. 517.

5 *One in Christ*, 1981, vol. 2, p. 102.

6 H. Volk, *Lexicon fur Theologie und Kirche*, vol. V, 1960, (2nd edn), vol. V, col. 641.

7 M. Schmaus, *Katholische Dogmatik*, 1965, vol. III/2, (6th edn), vol. III/2, p. 123.

8 Küng, *Justification*, p. 251.

9 *Theological Investigations*, vol. 4, p. 207.

10 *The Great Acquittal* (Collins Fount Original, 1980), 'Justification by Faith in Recent Roman Catholic Theology'.

11 *The Spirit and the Letter*, Library of Christian Classics, (SCM, 1955), vol. VIII, p. 241.

12 P. Blaser: quoted by Meyer, *One in Christ*, p. 104.

13 Council of Trent – English translation in *The Church Teaches*, (Burns and Oates, 1955), DS 1529.

14 Ibid, DS 1532.

15 *Theological Investigations*, vol. 4, pp. 205ff.

16 For example, E. Schillebeeckx, *The Tridentine Decree on Justification – a new view*, *Concilium*, vol. V, No. 1, p. 92f.

17 Trent, DS 1548.

18 Augustine, *De Gesms Pelagii*, chapt. xxxv.

19 Schillebeeckx, op. cit., p. 93.

20 O. Pesch, *Festschrift fur Schmaus*, 1967, vol. 2, p. 1867.

21 *Theological Investigations*, vol. 4, p. 221.

22 H. Friest quoted by Meyer, *One in Christ*, p. 103.

23 For an interesting comparison of the ecclesiologies of Vatican I and Vatican II see J. Tillard's article in *Irenikon*, 1980, (4) p. 451ff.

24 *The Passionist*, (SCM, London, 1976).

7. The justified minister at work

1 2 Cor. 3:9 (RSV): see also vv. 5 and 6.

2 See for instance Acts 8:4 and Peter's understanding of every Christian's role in 1 Pet. 2:9, 10.

3 Acts 2:38–40.

4 R. P. C. Hanson, *Eucharistic Offering in the Early Church*, (Grove Books, 1979), pp. 28–9.

5 A. W. Dale, *Life of Dr R. W. Dale,* (Hodder and Stoughton, 1889), p. 666.

6 J. Denney, *The Death of Christ*, new edn, (Tyndale Press, 1951), pp. 159–60.

7 Quoted from an interview recorded in *Ministry*, 1968.
8 H. J. M. Nouwen, *The Wounded Healer*, (Doubleday, 1972).
9 See 2 Cor. 2:17 and 3:5.
10 See Eph. 1:6.
11 Now printed as the first exhortation in the Communion service
   in the Book of Common Prayer (1662) – '. . . the way and means
   thereto (i.e. to being received as worthy partakers of that holy
   Table) is; first, to examine your lives and conversations by the
   rule of God's commandments . . .'
12 R. Foster, *Celebration of Discipline,* (Hodder and Stoughton,
   1980).
13 *The People's Penance Book*, (Redemptorist Publications, 1977):
   pages 10 and 11 of this booklet (headed Step Three: an Examination of Conscience) offer very helpful suggestions for any
   Christian to use in self-examination; a similar exercise from a
   different tradition can be found in W. E. Sangster, *A Spiritual
   Check-up*, (Epworth, 1952, and frequent reprints).
14 See the provision in the Prayer Book's service for the Visitation of
   the Sick, and the wording at the end of the exhortation mentioned in 11 above – '. . . if there be any of you, who by this
   means (i.e. self-examination, repentance, and, where appropriate, restitution) cannot quiet his own conscience herein, but
   requireth further comfort or counsel, let him come to me, or to
   some other discreet and learned Minister of God's Word, and
   open his grief; that by the ministry of God's holy Word he may
   receive the benefit of absolution, together with ghostly (i.e.
   spiritual) counsel and advice . . .'
15 Alternative Services, Second Series (revised), *Morning and Evening Prayer,* (CUP/Eyre and Spottiswoode/OUP/SPCK, 1970).
16 Owen, *Exposition of the Epistle to the Hebrews* (Thomas Tegg,
   London, 1840), vol. 1, p. 406.

8. Liturgy for the justified

1 G. Dix, *The Shape of the Liturgy*, (Dacre Press, 1945), p. 672.
2 Westminster Shorter Catechism.
3 Note especially in this connection Psalm 5.
4 Rev. 4:11.
5 Rev. 5:9–10, 12.
6 M. Perry, *The Paradox of Worship*, (SPCK, 1977), chap. 1.
7 Ibid, p. 5.

8 Neville Clark in *Worship and the Child* (Essays by the joint Liturgical Group), (SPCK, 1975), p. 67.

9 E. C. Whitaker, *Martin Bucer and the Book of Common Prayer* (Alcuin Club, 1974), p. 14.

10 *The First and Second Prayer Books of King Edward the Sixth* (Dent, 1910), p. 3.

11 R. P. C. Hanson, *Eucharistic Offering in the Early Church* (Grove Books, 1979), p. 29.

12 B. Spinks, *Luther's Liturgical Criteria and his Reform of the Canon of the Mass* (Grove Books, 1982), p. 31.

13 See for example Eph. 1:13, 14.

14 Opening verse of hymn 503, *Anglican Hymn Book,* by Horatius Bonar.

15 2 Cor. 5:21.

16 Hanson, op. cit., pp. 28–9. The whole section deserves careful study.

17 B. Spinks, op. cit., p. 37.

18 M. Marshall, *Renewal in Worship* (Marshalls, 1982), pp. 94–5.

19 For the way in which Cranmer intended this as a climax in the service see C. O. Buchanan, *What did Cranmer think he was doing?* (Grove Books, 1976).

20 From the hymn 'Rock of ages' by A. M. Toplady.

21 A. M. Ramsey, *Durham Essays and Addresses* (SPCK, 1957), p. 18.

22 ARCIC, *The Final Report,* (CTS/SPCK, 1982), p. 20.

23 *The Lambeth Conference 1958,* Report, (SPCK/Seabury), section 2.84–5, quoting Hebert's *Ways of Worship* (SCM, 1951).

24 R. Scott, 1912, see ch. 3.

25 B. F. Westcott, *The Epistle to the Hebrews* (Macmillan, 1889), p. 230.

26 P. E. Hughes, *A Commentary on the Epistle to the Hebrews* (Eerdmans, 1977), pp. 329–54.

27 1 Cor. 11:26, cf O. Cullmann, *Early Christian Worship* (SCM), and C. F. D. Moule, *Worship in the New Testament* (Lutterworth, 1961 and Grove Books, 1977–8).

28 Rev. 19:9.

29 For details of these see B. J. Wigan, *The Liturgy in English* (OUP, 1964), pp. 38–61.

30 M. H. Shepherd, *Anglican Congress 1954* (Eng. edn), p. 82, quoted in op. cit., section 2.83.

31 See p. 158 and note 12.
32 See the full text in M. Thurian and G. Wainwright (edd), *Baptism and Eucharist: Ecumenical Convergence in Celebration* (WCC/Eerdmans, 1983), pp. 249–55; also C. O. Buchanan, *ARCIC and Lima on Baptism and Eucharist* (Grove Books, 1983), pp. 17ff.
33 Quoted in J. H. Rodgers, 'Eucharistic Sacrifice: Blessing or Blasphemy', *Churchman*, 1964, vol. 78, pp. 248–54.
34 1 Cor. 11:26 (AV).
35 1 Cor. 15:3–5a.
36 J. I. Packer (ed), *Eucharistic Sacrifice* (CBRP, 1962), p. 149.
37 In ch. 5, pp. 104–7
38 1 Cor. 11:26.
39 Text taken from C. O. Buchanan (ed), *Further Anglican Liturgies 1968–1975* (Grove Books, 1975), pp. 191–2.
40 Heb. 4:14–16.